THE MASQUERADE IS OVER
Reclaiming You After Abusive Relationships

LUZELENIA CASANOVA

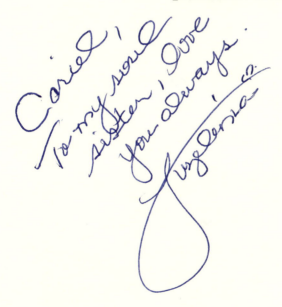

LC Influence
PO Box 1136
Chicopee, MA 01021

Limits of Liability and Disclaimer of Warranty
The author and publisher shall not be liable for your misuse of this material. This book is strictly for informational and educational purposes.

Warning – Disclaimer
The purpose of this book is to educate and entertain. The author and/or publisher do not guarantee that anyone following these techniques, suggestions, tips, ideas, or strategies will become successful. The author and/or publisher shall have neither liability nor responsibility to anyone with respect to any loss or damage caused, or alleged to be caused, directly or indirectly by the information contained in this book.

Copyright © 2011. All rights reserved. No portion of this book may be reproduced mechanically, electronically, or by any other means, including photocopying, without written permission of the publisher. It is illegal to copy this book, post it to a website, or distribute it by any other means without permission from the publisher.

ISBN-10: 0982733909
EAN-13: 9780982733905

DEDICATION

To my beloved sons Abraham and Kenneth, who continue to love me in spite of my mistakes and my poor choices in the past. You guys are my rock.

To my Heavenly Father and my Angels, for their divine assistance and giving me the courage in writing this book.

To all the victims of abuse who had the courage to leave the violence and make a better life for themselves and their children.

ACKNOWLEDGEMENTS

To the many people I would like to thank who were very instrumental in providing support and assistance in the writing of this book: Dr. Brader, Douglas Carroll, Seth Czerepak, Craig Duswalt, Jill McKellan, Scott Potter, Greg H. Stedman, Mark Steisel, and Melinda Thomas.

Special thanks to my dear friends who took time out of their busy lives to sit and proof my book. Thank you for providing valuable feedback: Ivette Castro , Cindy Columbia, Denise Moore, Marta Palermo, Milagros Rivera, Evelyn Turcotte, and Justina Vasquez.

To all my family and friends, including my Facebook peeps, for being my biggest fans in supporting me through this endeavor.

PREFACE

America is in the middle of a silent war, and millions of Americans are being held hostage each and every day. They are being beaten, abused, threatened, and killed. This war is difficult to fight and conquer because it takes place behind closed doors. Its victims remain paralyzed in fear, and feelings of helplessness and isolation are a part of their daily lives. The war is called domestic violence, and it's a vicious crime.

No one is safe from domestic violence; it creeps into your life slowly and takes over in the most manipulative way. It's in every community in America and across the world. Race, religion, gender, age, and wealth are irrelevant to the monster known as domestic violence. It considers everybody its prey. Domestic violence and abuse are not just for married couples either. It spills over into families, friends, coworkers, witnesses, and everybody who is close to it, infiltrated by its ugliness. It has even crept into our government and made them take action by creating services to help those who wish to conquer the ugly monster that is in their lives.

When a child grows up in a home where domestic violence is present, they are affected for their entire lives in their thought patterns and possibly even their actions as well. The physical and emotional trauma run deep within them and are difficult to still. The more they are exposed to such violence the more they are going to experience social, physical, and emotional problems. They soon start to see domestic violence as a way of life and view it as normal because they know no different. What does that mean? That means that if children do not learn a better way, they have a good chance of becoming the next generation of people who practice domestic violence and continue to accept it.

My crusade in life is to stop domestic violence from spreading out any further. My mission is to do everything within my power to help STOP the cycle of violence through four elements:

- Education
- Awareness
- Strength
- Courage

I invite you to join my crusade and fight side by side with me to eradicate the heinous and destructive plague that has waged war on all people here on earth. Remember, domestic violence is not particular, and it will take anybody in if they allow it.

In this book I will refer to domestic violence and domestic abuse. I am not only referencing what happens within the home. The terms are all-encompassing and include relationship violence of all sorts—harmful and abusive behavior that involves people in a relationship. That means that it is not just the family who can be catalysts for violent behaviors and tendencies. These vulgar evils can be found in relationships, friendships, business relationships, and social circles—not just within the family or home.

Introduction
MY STORY

This book is going to tell my experiences with domestic violence and the war it waged in my life, but it is written for you, your children, and those you love. The story is about the internal aspect of domestic abuse—a brutal and widespread crime. Domestic abuse is everywhere, and that means that its victims are everywhere as well. Sadly, there is always the chance that the victim will turn into the perpetrator because they know no different way. I invite everybody to work with me to stop that and take away the power that has been given to the vicious cycle of domestic abuse and how it trickles down from generation to generation.

This book will teach you about domestic violence as a whole, but it will also show you how to:

- Recognize it
- Learn about yourself
- Break the insidious cycle it breeds
- Reclaim and reinvent your life
- Learn to thrive after the abuse is over

For me, most of my life was spent being a victim of domestic abuse. It was a part of my earliest childhood memories and was present in my adult life too. My life was never a question of hearing that I was loved, rather showing me that I truly was loved. I feel action speaks louder than words. The people who claimed to love me also seemed to embrace the opportunity to beat me down emotionally, mentally, and physically. I've been through tremendous amounts of horrible pain and confusion, and as a result—self-hate.

I didn't gain the strength to stop the abusive patterns in my life for decades. I just coasted off of being emotionally beaten, bruised, and battered. Finally, I found the strength to eliminate it from my life. That moment was as frightening as it was liberating, and it took hard work to get there. I began to rebuild my life. In the process, I began to write this book. It was started with two purposes. The book has been an intricate part of my healing process, but it is also meant to be a tool to help others who may be feeling at their weakest from domestic violence right now. My story is not unique, but sadly, conquering domestic violence is far too unique.

This book has helped me evaluate my past and look at my life more objectively. The dedication that I have to understanding what has happened and what has resulted because of it will be my biggest defense in ensuring that I am never entangled in domestic violence again. Now I know what to look for, warning signs, and what I must avoid to win my personal war with domestic violence.

Thankfully, my story is a success story and a story about healing. I went from being an emotionally deprived child to a victimized adult. I always allowed others to make me miserable—like I didn't deserve better. Guess what? I realized that I do deserve better, and that's when I discovered and admitted that I had the power to stop the abuse from happening. I was in control of my life. Nobody else was going to take control of it for me and move me towards a positive direction. I hope that my pain can help others end their pain now or even help prevent it altogether.

The nightmare of domestic violence is bigger than all of us as individuals. However, as individuals who are united, we can come up with the solutions that will make a blueprint or template that can help others burst through the darkness of their abusive lives and see the brilliance of a life that is lived with love of self and lack of fear. You see, nobody was born to be abused or to be an abuser. That is nobody's destiny or greater purpose. Abuse is what stops people from reaching their potential and relishing in their abilities.

My Experience

The terms domestic violence and abuse bring up a very specific picture in a person's head. Most people think of physical harm and a person getting beaten up, having bruises, various black and blue marks, cuts, and even broken bones. Yes, that is true, but physical injuries are only a small part of the picture of domestic violence. Emotional, mental, and psychological abuses are equally damaging, sometimes even more so. They are not outwardly evident, but they eat away at people internally like the most deadly of diseases. Most types of domestic violence and abuse seem to court each other. In other words, most people will end up being victims of multiple forms of it. Any form of it is too much and must be eradicated from a victim's life.

I've suffered from both physical abuse and emotional abuse. Most of my suffering was caused by emotional abuse. That abuse eroded my self-confidence, destroyed my sense of self-worth, and shaped my feelings about myself and what I was capable of. The abuse told me I was weak and worthless. It caused me to believe that I was not entitled to a happy life. It limited my horizons and held me back from discovering my true potential, lest I leave and find my true path.

If you are reading this book and are a victim of any kind of abuse, I know how you've suffered, and I ache for you to find a way to get help. I've felt that same excruciating pain and torture—the kind that doesn't leave and never dulls, but constantly numbs you. I relate to your stories, excuses, anger, hate, fear, and shame. The only positive thing that comes from domestic violence is getting away from it when you have the opportunity. You have the opportunity today.

This book is a journey that will help you start to discover or rediscover your real self, your old self, and the self that was suppressed and basically forgotten. The self you put forth when you were being abused is not the self you were designed to be, and you'll gain the strength to see that and separate yourself from that stranger who was just trying to survive the circumstances. You are a survivor, and surviving takes strength, courage, and perseverance. It is what helps you summon up what you need to make changes even when you feel tired and weary from the battle. It's time to spark up your pilot light, stop being a victim, and transform your life.

I'm no longer a victim, and more importantly, I've learned not to think like a victim. The person I am is free to chart my own course. Since I've found the courage to leave my last abusive relationship, the prison I was sentenced to has gone away. I have discovered underlying strength and courage to help me bloom. I've finally become who I was born to be and learned how to reclaim my life and achieve more than I ever would have dared dream possible before. I've accomplished something incredible, and you can too. It's not exclusive to me, but it is all-inclusive for everybody who has been involved in the domestic violence war.

Today you have the opportunity to chart your own course and stop any cycle of abuse you may be in. You have the opportunity to give this book to somebody who is calling out for help. You have opportunity—plain and simple. Yes, this book is primarily written from one woman's perspective and life experiences, but it is invaluable to each and every person (man or woman) who is a part of the domestic violence cycle as either a victim or perpetrator.

> **Be Aware**
>
> Life may seem impossibly bleak and weary right now if you are in an abusive relationship. You may think hope exists for everybody else besides you. There is one thing you have to realize—the abuse is trying to keep control of you. It doesn't want you to become aware that you hold the power to stop it. You do, and your hope is just around the corner waiting for you to take the first step towards it. Get up, get moving, and make your escape.
>
> Once you are separated from days filled with fear of abuse and anger, you will see things much more clearly. It will be the most refreshing thought you've ever had. It's okay to be scared and nervous. It's not okay to let yourself be abused. Take a stand and start walking towards your new life that is free from abuse.

Did you know:

- Denial is natural.
- Excuses are natural.
- Domestic abuse and violence **are not natural!**

Believing in yourself and your ability to not only rebound but to rejoice in life is going to help carry you through your journey of leaving domestic violence. Your gut instincts are good, and you'll learn to trust them once again. You'll be shaky, you'll feel scared, and that is good—for many people that'll be the first time they've felt anything that leads to something positive for quite a long time. Leaving domestic violence is something that starts with baby steps and leads to growth that comes in leaps and bounds. Each step takes you closer to being the person you are supposed to be, want to be, and were meant to be.

Be courageous. Enjoy the freedom to live victoriously instead of continuing to be a victim. It takes courage to reinvent yourself after an abusive relationship, but you can do it. Be a scholar of your own life.

I'm still growing and blossoming. Today, I'm thankful to say that I cannot wait to see who I will become. The way I put it is "I'm a work in progress." That's because every day I have a learning experience and am introduced to something new. For the first time, as an adult, I have the confidence to know that my life is wonderful and that tomorrow will be even better. Since my life is rich and fulfilled, I would like to pass the lessons I've learned to you. I want to help you escape your pain and enjoy the wonders of life. Because, my friends, life is wonderful.

Enjoy the book. Read it, learn its lessons, reinvent yourself, and take off your mask. You are at home in these pages and accepted as the wonderful person you are. It's time to escape the pain and bondage of abuse and start to live. Let your strength and courage become your legacy to your children and loved ones. Do not give them the legacy of accepting violence, pain, and abuse.

Luzelenia Casanova
February, 2011

PART I
THE SILENT PATTERN OF ABUSE

Chapter One
THE LOVE OF A MOTHER

She should have been a vibrant, twelve-year-old girl playing mother with dolls. Instead, she was a barefoot and exhausted twelve-year-old girl who was forced to take care of her three younger siblings. She was one of eight children, and her mother relied on her to help as an adult. At the tender age of twelve, she was the disciplinarian and adult figure to those three small children. Her mother seemed to think she was a ball of fire and commanded the situation better than she could, so she handed over the duties of being a mother to her. She was reliable, loving, and fun—something her mother couldn't be to her.

This loving girl was just trying to be an important part of her mother's life and make her proud. School wasn't a priority for her mother because girls needed to become women who could manage a household, clean, and cook. That was what merited a good, strong woman. So my mother, this vibrant little twelve-year-old, cooked, ironed, cleaned, and cared for the other children as if they were her own. That is a lot of pressure for anybody. For a twelve-year-old girl, it was what she was determined to do so she could please her mother and feel loved by her.

My mother grew up trying to please her mother in every way possible. She was not the favorite child, but she soon became the slave of the family. She used to tell me that if she didn't follow the rules exactly, the consequences were severe and the punishment excruciatingly harsh. One of the more common punishments she would receive when she strayed from the path her mother chose for her was to have to kneel on raw rice in the corner for an entire day. My mother dreaded the punishment because her knees would start to bleed and her back would ache so severely. If she didn't maintain an erect back, her mother would pull out the paddle and take it to her butt until she regained her erect back.

My grandmother had also been abusive towards my mother and her siblings. Although it had never been talked about, my mother believed that her mother had also been abused. You see, it was one vicious cycle that was all-encompassing. So much anger and rage was in the family, and there was no way to release it except upon each other. My grandmother knew that she had a husband who was not faithful, and she cast the blame out to those around her because she was so angry about it.

Since my grandfather was never home and always busy chasing women, he was known around town for his activities. They called him the Don Juan of town because he was always wearing his fedora hat and pinstripe suit. My grandmother always complained that they barely had enough money for food, but he saw fit to buy sophisticated clothes to give an appearance of wealth. My mother used to laugh at how her father had fooled so many people. In reality, he couldn't afford more than the loaf of bread that was underneath his arm.

I admit that I was fascinated by my mother's stories. We would stand by the kitchen window and gaze out of it like we were in a dream. She'd be smoking and talking. It was our ritual, and I cherished it because that was one time when my mother was truly mine. Of course, I did choke from all the smoke fumes that billowed around the kitchen, but I didn't mind. The choking was worth having that little bit of time alone—just me and my mother.

Over the years I heard so many exciting stories about my mother's childhood. They seemed like wild tales and things that would never really happen. As I grew older, I realized that my mother had married the same type of man as my grandfather, and she was in full denial that she had turned into her mother. Her main focus was always my father's well-being, and that caused her to neglect us emotionally. She neglected herself even more and never tried to fulfill her own needs as a woman or a mother.

At the age of nineteen, my mother had fled her abusive home and moved to New York City with her older sister. She met my father five years after he moved to New York himself. They dated for a few months and then got married and moved to New Jersey.

My father was born in Puerto Rico. He had some demons of his own and had felt abandonment and neglect in his life. He'd been abandoned at birth because his birth mother was ashamed that his father was a married man. His relatives raised him for many years, and he bounced from one to the other at random. There was absolutely no stability or real home that my father could turn to. At fifteen he ran away from home and never returned.

Still, my parents did get married and must have loved each other somewhat, at least once upon a time. My mother was a hard worker, but she didn't work at anything nearly as hard as trying to win my father's love and affection. She tolerated his adulterous behavior, and I watched her desperately try to get him to love only her.

My mother had given herself the mission of saving my father and helping him heal from the pain he'd experienced from childhood. The problem was that nobody can heal somebody's pain if they aren't looking to be healed. She just couldn't accept that and was so angry because she felt she must not be good enough—that's why the pain wouldn't leave my father's heart and mind. She was so needy of his approval and never did find it.

I learned from my mother's behavior that the best way to get love was to be constantly needy and seeking approval. You couldn't be ignored then. Imagine my surprise when I finally realized that I had also followed my mother's and grandmother's pattern. It took me a long time to admit it, understand it, and decide to stop my self-destructive behavior. The process was long, miserable, and not easy. I'd had enough though and knew that I had to learn how to recondition my thinking. That would be achieved by reflecting back and finding out how I could move forward.

> *"We cannot hold a torch to light another person's path without brightening our own."*
>
> —Ben Sweetland

Chapter Two
AFFAIRS OF THE HEART

Everything we learn as children has the potential to become the gospel for our lives, what we always choose to accept as the truth. Parents are the greatest teachers a child will ever have. They influence our choices, decisions, and most of our beliefs and dreams. Through my life I've learned so many good things from my mother, but they were clouded by negative beliefs much of the time.

Despite the pain that my mother endured throughout her life, she could be such a compassionate, caring person. She was charitable and always found time to help others. She would feed the hungry, help the less fortunate, and have a kind word for them. Ironically, all that she gave to others she kept from her children. What we wouldn't have given to be one of her charitable cases at times.

My mother taught me humility, patience, empathy, and the importance of giving from the heart. Those are qualities that are deemed virtuous for any woman who's where I'm from. There are other qualities that are just the opposite of virtuous and good—my mother also taught me those. I learned to be vulnerable, submissive, needy, pessimistic, and codependent as well. As a child my dreams were squashed so I wouldn't get any false illusions of becoming somebody who could actually achieve something. My role in life was to fail and never lift myself up above the level of the most average Joe. There was no positive support system in place to let me or my siblings know that it was okay to dream big and go for it. I never knew I was good enough.

Suffering was not my burden to bear alone. My brothers also were forced to give up their dreams for mediocrity. My parents seemed to relish in the role of dream-killer for all of us. To encourage us to achieve something special for ourselves would have been impossible for them. They didn't seem to know how and certainly did not wish to try.

Both of my parents came from broken families and toxic environments. Neither one of them had ever learned to dream big or even believe it was acceptable to do so. They did what they knew best—live in fear of being poverty-stricken. Every single thing my parents did was based around their fear of not having enough to live on. Most people may think that fear would drive them to overachieve, but it didn't. It drove them to excel at safe mediocrity. Being under the radar and having no expectations placed on you to make the most of your gifts was not good. It was risky; therefore, it was bad.

My father was a brilliant man, despite his fears. He was a bus driver and a big saver. He invested in rental properties and made sure they produced a nice income for him. The people who knew him admired and respected his good business sense. Even with his financial smarts, he and my mother always considered themselves poor. They didn't believe they had a destiny to be anything more than poor people who just barely escaped poverty. Since they believed that was to be their destiny, they cast the same fate upon their children. In my parent's eyes, each and every one of their kids would also be poor because there was no other option. It was our destiny.

My brother was a very gifted athlete and was the star of his baseball team in high school. He had dreams of becoming a pitcher in the major leagues and really making a special career out of the sport he loved so much. The papers gave him accolades on a consistent basis, and everybody around him encouraged him to pursue his dreams of playing major league ball. I was so proud of him and thought it was absolutely incredible to have such a gifted brother. My parents, on the other hand, didn't give him any encouragement and tried to make him feel like his dreams were foolish and ridiculous. Eventually, they wore him down, and he enlisted in the navy. His passion shone through though, and he ended up in a rewarding career. And now he's also a coach who helps kids fulfill their dreams. I just loved seeing what happened for my brother despite my parents' fears.

As for me, my mother always claimed she knew I was going to be different and that I would come to reject the negative beliefs that were supposed to dictate my life. I think she always took my determination as judgment upon her, but it wasn't. She'd say things to me like, "You can act like an attorney, but you'll never be one." Human rights were always of interest to me, but I never saw that my role in helping was that of an attorney. You didn't need to have a law degree to passionately fight for what was right and considered basic human dignity. My childhood dream was to be a dancer.

Dancing was something that I loved so much, and I grew up with my idol being Iris Chacon. She was a flamboyant Puerto Rican dancer who pranced around the television stage in just her thong and exotic moves. It intrigued me that she was not thin, but rather curvy, vivacious, and totally sexy and unique. Back in the 1970s, her dancing was considered quite controversial. In its own unique way, I believe that Iris's show actually brought families together, if only for an hour a week. Men would rush home to see her, and women would be thankful and prepare big meals to celebrate a real family night. For that moment many wives simply had to accept the fact that they were gathered to watch a half-naked woman dance for their husbands—thankfully on TV.

If you've never heard of Iris Chacon, you should check her out on YouTube. It would be mild by today's standards, without a doubt, but you'd be able to see what I meant. I was eight years old and trying to learn some of those wild moves that I saw every week. I would laugh and do them for my mother's friends when they came over. They all thought it was good, harmless fun, but I later found out that my mother thought I was committing a sin.

One of my mother's friends, Petra, was like a second mom to me. She often gave me the attention that my mother didn't. There was a Puerto Rican festival going on in our neighborhood, and she asked my mom if she could take me. It was simply exciting and exhilarating that she let me go, and I was so very thankful. For one of the first times in my life I was going to get to see live music, go on rides, and play games. What a fantastic day it would be.

The festival was very crowded. I could barely see over all the people, and the amazing smells of authentic Spanish food floated in the air as my feet danced with excitement. Since I still wanted to be a dancer so bad, I was absolutely delighted to be by the rhythmic music and absorbed it all in. An announcement rang out over the crowd. There was going to be a dance contest. There was no thinking twice—I eagerly wanted to enter that contest. Maybe it would be the lucky break to make my eight-year-old dreams come true. I asked Petra if I could enter it, but she was very hesitant. She knew that my mother would never approve of such a thing and didn't want to overstep her boundaries on our outing. Those moments when Petra hemmed and hawed over if she should let me enter quickly came to a close. I had been dancing in place waiting for her answer, and one of the judges saw me. They pointed to me and said, "Let's get this young lady in the contest!"

There are thrilling moments, and then there are extra spectacular thrilling moments in life. That moment fell into the latter category for me. I was so excited to get up on that stage and was set to dance with all my heart and soul and win that contest. I was positive that Iris Chacon would have been very proud of me, had she been there. I shook my little booty around and played to the crowd like I was a professional. I won the dance contest and couldn't have been more proud. The prize was a trophy of a tall, statuesque woman with her arms extended over her head and beautiful wings extended out around her. They reminded me of what angel wings must look like. The excitement of the moment was so incredible, and for the first time in my young life I really felt like I'd achieved something big—something important.

My elation quickly came to a screeching halt when I got home. Suddenly the trophy I had been so proud of minutes before was going to be the inspiration behind a major punishment with a belt. My mother was so angry, and she was waiting for me with that belt in her hand. She'd already heard that I had been dancing like Iris Chacon at the festival and believed that such flamboyant dancing in the street was degrading and disgusting. There was no opportunity for explanation or anything. My mother started beating me with that belt so savagely.

As the pain surged through my body, I realized that I was still holding my trophy. As the blows viciously struck me, the trophy was released from my grip and went flying into the air. It was like slow motion, and I remember every thought, every movement very vividly to this day. My beautiful trophy was flying through the air and plunged to the floor, and both of those beautiful angel wings were shattered to bits.

The days after that brought so many painful tears for so many reasons. I cried for the broken wings on my trophy. I cried because I was in pain, and I cried because I didn't understand my mother's awful wrath against me. When I look back on it today, I can realize that it wasn't the prize that made me cry. It was my broken heart and the symbolism of smashing my dreams of being able to dance.

When my mother destroyed my dream, it felt like the end of my world at that moment. My miserable perception ruled my outlook on everything. Life became nothing but a grim, hopeless burden that I'd have to face with no promise of joy or laughter. I kept reliving the moments of that festival day, and each time I went through a personal journey to hell and back. I found that the only way I could not feel so miserable was to adopt my parents' way of thinking. There was no choice besides accepting that my dreams were unrealistic and had no chance of coming true. It was time to settle for what life dealt me and stop thinking that my potential was for anything more.

Wifely Loyalty

One of the most glaringly obvious, yet highly confusing things that my mother did was show the clear differences between what would be tolerated from her children and her husband. We each were given a separate set of guidelines to live by in my mother's world.

My mother made it very clear that there would be no dreaming for my siblings and me. We were not destined to do great things and should make everyone's life easier by just putting those ridiculous thoughts out of our minds. We were not special and shouldn't make fools out of ourselves by trying to act that way.

My father lived by a code of infidelity and didn't care about the harm it caused. My mother was always understanding, loyal, and devoted to him despite it. She would have done anything my father asked and always did even though it often caused her both physical and mental harm.

The one and only love of my mother's life was my father. That sounds like it should be wildly romantic and the stuff that true love is made of. With them it was everything but that. My mother generously gave her freedom and self-respect just to keep my father with her. She relied on him to do anything and thrived on being dependent on him, as if that dependency was the magic formula to keeping them married. She never learned how to drive, shop for food by herself, or manage any money at all.

Submissiveness was a plague that festered in my childhood home for as long as I could remember. It was highly infectious, and everybody was susceptible to it. For me, it was normal and just the way life was. I had no idea it could be any different inside the walls of a home. That belief robbed me of my freedom and independence for a long time.

It's so difficult to see when you are in a situation, but our beliefs are fostered from the moment we are born and cultivated by our parents throughout our lives. Teachers and other kids also play a critical role. So if by chance you are surrounded by toxic thinkers, you really believe it is just the way you are supposed to think. We learn from everything around us, and everything has the potential to significantly impact our lives. If the lessons are constantly negative, they soon go on autopilot, and people find out that they are skeletons walking through life with no passion or purpose. It's so sad to see and something that is hidden in the subconscious.

Everybody owes it to themselves to examine their beliefs and where they stem from. That is the only way to determine if they are healthy and geared towards leading you to a prosperous, healthy life. If you don't believe that your belief system generates positive things, then you need to reboot it. Find the good in life so you can start living it. That is how you will chart your own course and becomes the person you wish to be.

"As he thinks in his heart, so is he."

—Proverbs 23:7

Chapter Three
PAWNS OF MENTAL ABUSE

Some of the most substantial pain we can experience in our lives comes from what happens to us within, not just physically. Playing with people's minds without physically touching them can be harsher than the deepest of cuts you may physically receive. They can last forever and are often hidden deep inside of you, resulting in fear, insecurity, and self-loathing.

Through my childhood I witnessed and experienced so much mental abuse. At times I was the target, and other times I was put in the middle of my parents' battles and used ruthlessly against each other. One summer really stands out for me. I was eleven years old, and my parents had been separated for three months. One morning my father called our home to speak with my mother. She wasn't there—she was outside by a neighbor's house. He asked me who she was with, and I told him, thinking nothing of it. After I mentioned the neighbor man's name, my father abruptly hung up the telephone without so much as another word.

Since I didn't understand what was going on, I decided to go let my mother know that my dad had called. I went out and told her. I remember saying, "Daddy just called." It was a simple and harmless fact to me. To my mom it was obviously something else.

She snapped at me harshly and said, "I hope you didn't tell him where I am or who I'm talking with."

Obviously, I had to tell my mother that I had indeed mentioned both of those things. She got so upset and started screaming at me hysterically. Until that very moment I had no idea that my father disliked the neighbor man that my mother was speaking with. My mother didn't calm down and kept up her ranting. My father drove up.

My father's car screeched to a halt, and he jumped out quickly. The car was half in the street, and the driver's side door was wide open. My mother ran into the house, and my father raced in after her. I was so confused about what was happening and tried to follow in the house after them. When I got to the top of the stairs going into the house, I stopped. My mother was screaming.

Her shrill and panic-stricken voice was ringing through the house from the kitchen. I quickly ran through the kitchen door because I was so scared that she was getting hurt. When I got through that door, however, I saw something very different. My mother had a large kitchen knife in her hand and was trying to stab my father. I was simply horrified. I started screaming, "Don't kill my daddy." I'm not sure how many times I yelled it, but I know I kept repeating it.

The screaming eventually did distract my mother, and my father grabbed her wrists. He was a towering six feet tall and was able to keep her at arm's length. That didn't stop my mother, though. She was a force to be reckoned with and refused to give up the fight. She didn't stop struggling, yelling, kicking, and trying to stab my father. My father had no choice but to squeeze her wrist very tightly in hopes that she would have to drop the knife. It didn't work, and she held onto the knife like it was glued to her. Then she noticed me.

The struggle continued in the kitchen that day. My mother turned to me while struggling with my father. She had such hate in her eyes and a ferocious look that sent chills down my spine. She shouted to me, "Keep defending him. You're going to end up leaving with him too." I couldn't say anything and didn't know what to do. I was too scared to try and help either of them. Thankfully, a neighbor came into the kitchen.

The neighbor told both my parents that she was calling the cops. At that point my father backed away from my mother and let her go. He quickly turned around and hightailed it out of the house. Apparently, he was not about to be involved in any altercation with the police, and I was thankful for that too.

As a result of the occurrence, my mother suffered two fractured wrists. The blame for the injury was cast upon me, and my mother had no problem reminding me that she felt it was my fault. If I hadn't told my father that she was talking to that neighbor man outside, then none of it would have happened. I became convinced that my mother was right and it was my fault. I bought her version and accepted all the blame. I really believed that I was an awful daughter and had betrayed my mother. Worse than the betrayal, I had caused her harm.

Feeling that I had done that to my mother caused me to take action. I wanted to make things right and dedicated myself to saving my parents' marriage. Since I was the cause of their problems, I knew I had to make some changes so they could get back together. I begged and pleaded with my father to move back home and was relentless in trying to convince my mother to agree.

My determination to correct my wrongs won out. Within a month my father moved back home, and my mother took him back. They still fought, and my father still cheated. My mother always kept me in check by reminding me of all the troubles I had caused too. The guilt trip to make me believe that it was my responsibility to make their marriage work lasted for a long time. It took even longer for me to admit that it wasn't my fault at all.

Both of my parents didn't hesitate to use my guilty feelings against me. I was always manipulated by both of them. I was put in the middle of their adult issues, and if I had a question each would send me to the other to find out. I was even asked to spy on my father by my mother. Since I was a kid, I just kept trying to do what everybody asked because I didn't know what else I could do. I was desperately fighting to try and keep my family intact.

Parental Abuse

Few parents ever intentionally place their children in the middle of their difficult, adult situations. It still tends to happen more than it ever should. Some parents make an art form out of making their children feel responsible for matters that they did not cause and certainly cannot control. When they do that, they cause confusion and fear in their kids. The guilt a child can feel for believing they've caused their parents' problems can be overwhelming and burden them more than they should ever have to experience. Children are not equipped emotionally or mentally to handle such terrible emotional abuse. It is a betrayal on the parents' part to put them into that difficult position.

Children were never intended to be pawns in adult affairs and problems. Making them a pawn is a very serious form of abuse that should never happen. It leaves lasting scars and teaches children the wrong lessons for dealing with problems in life with a healthy perspective. Manipulation, blame, and guilt are not actions and feelings that children should be associated with—ever. Children who are victims of those things grow up to be parents who repeat those actions. Nobody wins when that happens. It is up to each adult to take responsibility for their life and stop the vicious cycle of casting blame on innocent children.

Don't put children in adult positions. They can't handle it, and it's not fair to them. Not only can't they solve their parents' problems, they can end up taking on lots of new and unnecessary problems of their own.

Chapter Four
THE BEGINNING OF THE END

When I first heard that my mother had cancer, I was in denial. That is not uncommon, but I just couldn't believe it. She was always so proud, and to hear her admit that she had any weakness was amazing. I just kept saying that I thought she should get a second opinion. There was no other choice. Of course she refused. She'd always prided herself on not going to doctors and would share how the last time she had seen one was when I was born. In hindsight, I should have realized that meant she knew something was definitely wrong. Why else would she ever go back to a doctor and ruin her record? Denial is a friend to people who don't want to face reality. I became very close with denial over the years.

My mother knew something was wrong when she started to have excruciating pain in her leg. It got to the point where she could barely walk without problems, and that's when she caved in and went to the doctor. The doctor told her that she had stomach cancer. She thought he was full of crap and refused to believe him. He wanted her to have surgery and chemotherapy, and she refused treatment. Her attitude was, "Everyone's got to die someday, and my turn is coming soon!"

My mother's turn came quite quickly. Within six months she lost over forty pounds and weighed a fragile eighty pounds. She was only sixty-seven years old, but she looked eighty years old. It was hard to believe that she was the same woman capable of putting such fear in me all those years.

The cancer rapidly made its home in my mother's body and spread like wildfire. It was believed that the cancer had been there for a few years, but it went without the necessary treatment and detection due to my mother's adamant beliefs that doctors were of no use to her. Well, that mindset had caught up to my mother. She finally caved in when it was too late for effective treatments and possible remission. Her vanity and pride had been the factors that contributed to her ultimate demise. Her belief that showing you were sick was a sign of weakness ended up sealing her fate with her cancer.

My brothers and I had been through an entire life hearing, "What would people think?" It was one of my mother's most favorite questions, and she asked it all the time. None of us dared answer it though because it was really meant to be more of a statement. As a result, we led lives designed to keep up appearances, look good, and save face at all costs. We were continually reminded that everything we did was a reflection on her, so we'd better not mess up. My siblings and I did everything possible to ignore our instincts and impulses and just do what would make my mother happy. The problem was that nothing made her happy because she wasn't happy and didn't know how to go about trying to be.

My mother didn't like it, but she finally had to put her pride aside because the fact that she was very ill could not be hidden. Thankfully, everybody who knew her knew that consoling her was a big no-no. We all knew they did so behind her back though, and I imagine she did too. If they would have shown her pity (or us, for that matter) my mother would have been livid and used her last bits of energy to put her wrath out there on the violators of her pride. So, in the tradition of her unhealthy thinking and lifestyle, my mother isolated herself and refused to visit or be visited. She preferred loneliness that held her pride intact to the companionship of people who genuinely cared.

Forgiveness

For all the anger and unhappiness that my mother had always held within, she did teach her kids one very valuable lesson. That lesson was that in order to die in peace, people must resolve their conflicts and disputes with others. Without forgiveness and clearing the slate, there was no dying in peace. It is probably not surprising to hear, but my mother liked to preach that message to others more than live it. She carried vendettas to her grave and refused to forgive a good many people whom she felt had wronged her in her life.

Since my mother was on her deathbed, I thought it was important for her to repent and forgive. For both our sakes, I needed her to forgive me, and I wanted her to know that I forgave her. I knew that I harbored anger and resentment towards her, and I wanted to forgive her. There was no other option for me. I wanted a happy and fulfilled life and did not want to live in the sadness my mother had managed to survive in.

> *"If you forgive other people their failures,*
> *your Heavenly Father will also forgive you.*
> *But if you will not forgive…neither will your Heavenly*
> *Father forgive you of your failures."*
>
> —Matthew 6:14–15

Even though we hear and understand the importance of forgiveness, it is still amazingly difficult to do. Over the course of my life, when I've asked friends to forgive somebody who has hurt them I usually hear, "No. I'm not letting them get away with it!" People don't realize that forgiveness is a gift to yourself more than it is a gift to others. What is inside of you is what you can control.

When you forgive, it releases your pain and makes you stronger. The resentment I'd been harboring against my mother was long and deep. It hadn't hurt her—it had hurt me. In fact, I was weakened because it gave her the power to control my emotions. I made a conscious decision that I wasn't going to have my anger interfere with and spoil the remaining time I had with my mother.

At Her Bedside

There was no denying that the end was growing near. It felt awkward to be faced with such a harsh reality when denial had been embraced by me and my family for so long. I decided to take some time off from work so my mother wouldn't have to be alone. I slept next to her in a recliner and cherished all the moments that I was having with her. At times, I found myself praying and wishing it was me lying there in that bed and not her. I wanted God to take her pain away and not bring her to his home. She had grandchildren to enjoy and people who still needed her here on earth.

One night we sat in the dark chatting. She asked me if I thought she was going to die. My heart said yes, but my head fought back with a determined no. I wasn't sure what to say, so I threw the question back at her. She hesitated at first and eventually replied. "I know I'm dying because your father [who had been dead for several years] has been coming to the room every night and sitting down to wait for me."

I asked, "Mom, are you afraid of dying?" She hesitated, unsure how to answer, and finally she said, "Yes, how do you know?" I told her that I could hear it in her voice and sense it.

In that tender moment with my mother, I got a bit braver and asked her, "Are you ready to surrender your life to God?" She refused to answer me and turned around to sleep.

For a brief second I had wondered why I'd failed in that moment and thought it may have been better to not bring it up. I didn't mention it again, but I certainly didn't give up hope either. I wanted her to surrender so badly. One day she finally declared it to me and more importantly to God. "I'm ready to surrender!"

That moment was so exciting and profound. My friends and the pastor came to celebrate, and we were all excited about her new freedom. She said she felt such a great feeling and a sense of peace and joy. It was something she'd never experienced before.

Everything that happened in those two weeks gave me hope. I felt she was given a second chance at life—a new beginning. I promised God that I would forgive my mother and start anew with her. That evening we cried in each other's arms. It was the most love I'd ever felt from my mother, and I feel its warmth to this day. It was there, on her deathbed, that her deprived and love-starved child finally received what she needed. That attention and love was something that was no longer withheld, but there to enjoy and revel in.

I went back home because I felt my mother was doing better and that God had heard my plea for a second chance and was giving it to me.

Two weeks later I was called back to the hospital. When I got there nobody needed to say a word. Death was lingering in the air in that hospital room. The second I walked in there I knew that a major part of what had been distressing in my life was leaving. I could just feel it. I looked over and saw the shell that used to be my mother lying there with her eyes closed and no longer living in this world.

Reflections of the Past

The emotions and thoughts were overwhelming as they swirled around me. I became dizzy and felt like I was tumbling down a mountain in an avalanche. It was frightening, overwhelming, and numbing. Tears started to fall from the corners of my eyes, and my body shook. As to the source of my tears, I couldn't say for sure. Part of the tears may have been from relief; the other source of those tears was genuine grief for the loss of a woman whom I had always wanted to love me and accept me. I'd dreamt of that for many years. It would never happen now, and I couldn't help but reflect on the lost opportunities on both our sides.

Just as quickly as the dizziness came the anger arrived. For years I'd felt like I was being suffocated underwater and having the life snubbed out of me by this woman. She had kept me wrapped in the fury of her personal storm for as long as I had been alive. I was frustrated for so many reasons—the loss, the longing, and the guilty joy of peace for myself. Finally, my tumultuous relationship with my mother was over. I was released by her death.

As I stared at her lifeless body, I wondered if she would ever rest in peace. I hoped that she had finally found the place where she could be happy, content, and maybe a bit proud of me. After all, that was all I'd ever wanted.

The thoughts that swirled through my mind came in jumbled spurts. I felt grief, devastation, and something that I thought may be close to relief. I tried to make sense of my feelings, but I wasn't sure how to go about it. I had just lost my closest relative, but she was also the worst tormentor I'd ever had in my life. How do you deal with that and handle it? I wasn't sure I knew how and didn't know how to ask anybody else about it, lest they think I was a heartless child.

The shell of my mother didn't look like the diabolical, abusive tormentor I'd known my entire life. She looked like a sad, lonely, and washed-up woman. It was so utterly confusing, and I just wanted to picture a woman who was all good all the time. I desperately reached into my memories for the times when my mother actually showed warmth, caring, and kindness. Those moments had been there, but I had a difficult time finding them. The intensity of the cruelty that had caused me so much devastation was too strong an emotion and wouldn't allow for anything besides loathing to surface.

I don't believe that I was being irrational in wondering how anybody who claimed to love me could seem to indulge in all the pain they caused me. It took me years of therapy and growth to start realizing that she just hadn't known any other way. My mother had never had a life where she felt truly loved or appreciated, and that was very sad. It must have been very lonely. It was not, however, an excuse for being cruel to a child and stripping her of self-esteem and the courage to flourish in life.

The weeks immediately following my mother's death brought on an onslaught of denial about the fact that she was really gone. When the phone would ring, old habits would automatically cause me to think that it was my mother calling to criticize me or remind me of my failed marriage and how much she hated my current husband. The insanity just never stopped with my mother, and I couldn't do a darn thing about it. Now the phone was silent, and I'd never have to hear her stinging words again about any of my perceived shortcomings in her eyes.

Of course, my mother did give me enough sugar and honey to keep me hanging on. It was if she had a gauge by her telephone that said she'd went too far and had better do some good so she could use it up once again with cruelty. The cycle was so crazy, and I just never did have the strength to keep up with it. Yet, every time she did say something good, I held on to that and the way it made me feel. Even though she was cruel more often than not, I longed for those kind words. When they came, I was like a kid at Christmas—so excited and optimistic, if only for a minute.

And that, my friends, was the beginning of the end.

PART II

SEARCH FOR MY IDENTITY

Chapter Five
BROTHERLY LOVE

The questions that have stormed my brain and constantly challenged me with doubt about who I really am and I was meant to be tormented me for years. I've never known how to answer and felt like I was walking aimlessly with no sense of self or purpose. I relied on my brothers to protect me and provide emotional support I desperately needed.

After high school I wanted to go away to college. My mother told me that was not an option in no uncertain terms. The only path of escape I had from my house was if I got married, and that decision really tore at my heart and emotions. All I wanted was to go to college, and the thought of going into a marriage was terrible and very saddening. There was an amazing world out there to explore, and I was stuck in a glass ball getting teased by all the things that—according to my mother—were not meant for me to enjoy.

My mother had always been the rule-setter in our home, and my father never had a say in family matters. She always claimed to have a reason for all her madness, but I often wondered what it was. When I was a teen, she tried her best to control every aspect of my life. I couldn't work because it would ruin my school grades and I may become too independent. I couldn't date because she insisted I was too young and I must be kept on a short leash. I was able to have a boyfriend on occasion, but once they realized that I had a very strict mother, they would disappear and no longer be interested.

After high school, despite my mother's adamant protests, I enrolled in a local business school and weighed my options on what I wanted to do. It was becoming increasingly unbearable to live with my mother, and I stood no chance of pleasing her with any decisions I made. I really wanted to work and earn my own money while I was in school. She thought that was ridiculous and unacceptable. Finally, she decided that if I did take a job it must be nearby.
The identity crisis that my mother helped create didn't stop at just me. It manifested itself in my brothers as well.

My Brothers

Our family consist of two older brothers and myself, I was the only daughter and youngest child. It would be expressing it mildly if I said that I had kind of a love/hate relationship with my mother. My brothers had always made me feel protected no matter what, and I valued that protection with all my heart. Whenever my mother beat me, they would step in and tell her to stop. My mother didn't like that my brothers protected me, and once in a while she'd even have them discipline me. I could see in their eyes that there was no choice; they had to do it. Since both my older brothers left home at a very young age, I felt abandoned by them somewhat. I had counted on them to help protect me and soon found that I had no defense from my mother's actions and how they impacted me.

My oldest brother left home when he was fifteen. He received a scholarship to attend an accelerated high school in New Hampshire that was for gifted students. He was a brilliant kid who never missed school and always got straight As. His discipline was something to be admired. My father verbally and physically abused him. When he was young, he had the ability to stay focused on what he wanted and dig deep down and not let it ruin his course. He ended up never returning home after college and joined the army. Once he experienced the freedom that came from not being at home, he couldn't go back.

My other brother was the rebel of the family, but he always respected my mother. He lived by his own rules and didn't always follow my mother's rules. If she said he couldn't do something, he'd find a way to sneak off when she wasn't paying attention. When he was not allowed to go out, he'd jump out his bedroom window down into our neighbor's backyard and cross over their fence and come back the same way. Just think of Spiderman and how he can maneuver any building and you'd have a great picture of what my brother was like.

My younger brother finally reached his breaking point and had enough. He came home one day and discovered that my father had sold his car with everything in it to a stranger. And by everything I mean the brand new stereo he installed and very proud of and all his baseball equipment too. That was it, and it really toppled my brother emotionally. He felt like his world was over. Baseball was his life, and he was so talented at it. He wanted to get away and was willing to sacrifice his dreams to do so. He turned down a baseball scholarship because it was too close to home and enlisted in the navy. He saw that as his only way out. Thankfully, everything worked out great for him.

Left Alone

After my brothers left, I really fell into a rut with my parents. They were so difficult to deal with, and I constantly felt isolated, aimless, and bullied. My mother remained leading an angry, bitter life with my father. My father continued to be gone all the time. He had two jobs and spent time with other women when he wasn't working. He made no time to be home with my mother, and that made her take out her anger on me. I was the only one at home with her, and I was constantly subject to her abuse.

Despite the intense pain I felt, I also felt conflicted. I felt an urgency to help my mother, and I would try for awhile. Then I'd grow impatient because my mother was determined to do everything she wanted to do and I should stick by her side regardless of what she did. It was so painful and frustrating, and I felt completely trapped. I felt like a trapped animal in a cage, like the lion at the circus.

One day, my lion tamer showed up. There he was waiting for me—an abuser with a mental whip. I was so broken from my mother's abuse and didn't see the signs clearly at all. They were certainly there, but I justified ignoring them at the time because it was still an out from my current painful life.

My soon-to-be husband came from a family that was just as dysfunctional as mine. I didn't fall in love with him right away, but I eventually broke down. In fact, I'd kindly rejected his advances repeatedly. He just wasn't my type. There was always something that I couldn't name that made me uncomfortable. Unfortunately, I found out that his obsessive tendencies were a huge problem far too late. I'd caved in and finally accepted his advances and saw him as my ticket to freedom. I ignored his behaviors and focused on his physical appearance. He was very handsome.

Many women believe that they can change the behaviors of men they love if they just show them devotion and love. I was no different with my new love. I praised him, and he preyed on my needy behaviors. The funny thing was, I also believed he could fix me and make me whole for once. I was so starved for love and affection that I ate it all up when it came to him. I couldn't get enough, and he kept feeding me more just to keep control of me.

My soon-to-be husband was younger than me, but he acted so much older. He had street smarts, a macho attitude, and was an exciting bad boy from New York City—and he loved me! It was wildly romantic and made me believe that I'd finally receive the love and attention that had never been given to me growing up. I came to find out that what I once saw as strength and bravery was an illusion for a pathetically egotistical, self-centered, weak man.

Chapter Six
THE SILENT CYCLE

My future husband courted me passionately. It was the first time I had ever received so much attention in my life from somebody, and the way he expressed his love eventually captured me. Initially, I was hesitant to accept this man's advances because I didn't have a good vibe about him at all. There was only so much resistance in me though. After we got married, he continued to be romantic. I'd get cards, stuffed animals, and handwritten poems.

The way my mother adored him intrigued me. She saw him as the faithful, passionate man she never had. I should have been worried about my mother thinking he was so spectacular, but admittedly he won me over with his charismatic charm too. The attention was absolutely mesmerizing and so foreign to me. I built him up in my head to be the ideal, but eventually I was forced to take the blinders off and stop living in a fantasy.

My Mr. Ideal started to show signs of being obsessive and possessive. At first I said it was deep love and devotion. Soon it escalated to unjustified jealousy that was slowly growing out of control. This all happened before we were even married. He would call me ten to fifteen times a day at home. If I didn't answer, he'd drive all the way from New York City to New Jersey and wait by my home until I arrived.

The obsessive behavior soon grew to be too much for me. One night he even sat outside in his car all night long after I broke up with him. He vowed to stay there until I took him back, so I did. My mother was so furious with me and couldn't believe I'd be so cruel to him. She reminded me that I'd be a stupid fool if I let him go because he was a good, devoted man.

I soon discovered that taking him back meant that I was contributing to his behavior and enabling him. Without even realizing it, I had given him permission to not trust me and manipulate me constantly. The harsh reality of the fact that this man didn't love me so much as he loved possessing me was evident. Still, I didn't want to admit it.

Over time, our relationship got worse because in order to keep him from getting angry, I made sure to always be available for him. No matter what I should be doing, I made sure I was right there for him first. It was easier than having a confrontation or situation. Unfortunately, logic is not the friend of disturbed people. The more I tried to show my loyalty, the worse he became.

Trust is supposed to be the key to any successful relationship. Without it the relationship cannot work. If one partner doesn't trust the other, problems are going to arise. The baggage people bring to a relationship doesn't help. Suddenly you become the person they used to be with in a prior relationship. They couldn't trust that person, and now they can't trust you because of that person in the prior relationship. It's a vicious cycle which will lead you on the road to nowhere—lost time, bad memories, and a messed up sense of self-worth.

When you reflect back on your life when you were with an abusive person, it is so much clearer to see the error in hindsight. I should have been wise enough to never accept the man, but I wasn't. Just to ensure he had his snares entangled around me more tightly, he romanced me more and I got pregnant. We were not married, and I was certainly not ready to be a mother. I was terrified. When I told my mother about it, she insisted that we wed, and I listened. I didn't feel like I had any other choice at that point.

The entire time I was married it was destructive in every way possible. We were so addicted to each other. It made it impossible for us to be together and equally impossible to be apart. We'd separate, and he'd immediately dive into another relationship. He usually moved in with the woman. Then he'd come back and woo me, we would be intimate, and he would tell me that he had changed. Of course he always managed to add lines like, "We are still married, and you are my wife." Every time I fell for it. I felt hopelessly pathetic and stupid. Where was my toughness and backbone? Why couldn't I tell that man no once and for all?

When you are in an abusive relationship, patterns tend to repeat themselves. They still catch you off guard every time though. I suppose it's that glimmer of hope that helps you survive day to day. It sure was for me at times. Women often leave their abusers only to return later. They come and go multiple times until something snaps and it ends. Truth be told, it should have ended in the beginning.

As I recall the endless times my parents fought, it makes my head spin. I remember how much I despised it, but I still managed to do that myself. My poor son's head probably spun as much as mine did over all the confusion. It was fairly surreal that I had become my mother since I had always had the determination to not be like that.

My mother did not see anything wrong with my husband at the time. She thought he was good and kind. The reminders that it was my duty to preserve my marriage—REGARDLESS—were always present and an undertone in her words. She never understood why I would kick him out when the problems we were having were, in her opinion, my fault. Since I was the one making him angry, it was my job to make amends with him.

That marriage lasted eleven years. I can't recall the exact number, but I know we separated at least six times during those eleven years. Each one lasted three months at the most. The addiction to the abusive relationship would not let either of us stop the insanity. We kept holding on and pulling each other back. Neither of us wanted to admit failure, and so we took the prideful struggle instead. During the last four years of the marriage, it turned violent. By that time, I was so emotionally damaged that my self-esteem and self-confidence were dangerously low. I just clung to the sickness in front of me because I couldn't find the strength to let go. I stayed addicted to the relationship and the abusive behavior. He ate away at my soul until I got to the point where I felt none was left.

Chapter Seven
LULLABY BABY

It all started out seeming like a very kind gesture. I was wrong. After we got married, my father rented us a townhouse with a door that provided access to their home. That door was located in our bedroom. To this day, I see that door as a symbol of the separation it caused my family in multiple ways.

The time after my first son's birth was blissful. Everyone was delighted and enjoyed having this amazing little baby in their lives. My son brought renewed energy and excitement that had been lacking for quite some time. He was my parents' first grandchild and my dad's hope for somebody he could influence to be a Yankees fan. I would watch my father with fascination. It was the first time I'd ever seen him show any other person emotion or affection.

My mother thought my son would be a good source of distraction for her. She took over full control of him and discredited my skills as a mother from the very start. Considering whom I learned parenting from that may have been true. She would reprimand me for leaving my son crying for too long. If he cried, she rushed over and told me what I should be doing. Basically, my mother did what she does best—belittle me, insult me, and express that I lacked competence.

We never had the conversation, but I always had a feeling that my mother took over control of my son because she was trying to make up for what she was not to me. She would cuddle him close and glowed with happiness about having such a healthy little grandson. Parts of me envied and ached because I knew that I had never received such a warm look from my mother in my entire life. It was very painful, and I had to view it like a stranger looking in at a family through a window. You know, you envy something that looks ideal, but you've never experienced. Why couldn't my mother have been just a fraction of that woman with me?

Over time, my mother's obsession with my son crossed the line and became overwhelming. To make it worse, my son adored her and often chose her over me when he needed comfort, joy, and a hug—anything, really. He was very young, but I could see how my son manipulated his grandmother to get his way. I suppose any child may be that way, but he was surrounded by others who knew how to manipulate all too well. It was frightening. In the end, it caused a divide between my family members.

My brothers would watch her coddle my son and complain because he was too spoiled. Anything he said went, and he knew that Grandma would throw anybody under the bus if they caused him distress. He was so self-centered and indulgent in life. It was obvious that he was starting off on shaky ground and not building a life upon a solid foundation.

I found myself in a toxic home for the second time in my life. I was always on edge, and it felt like I lived in an occupied country. If I made one false move, I'd be punished in the most terrible way. It was insane to see that I was a wife, a mother, and still completely under my mother's control and subject to her rules—plus my husband's rules.

There are few things that are more heart-wrenching than feeling helpless as a mother and a wife. Nobody gave me a chance, and I didn't know how to go about creating my own chance. My mother dictated my life, along with the help of my husband. I didn't have the strength to deal with them separately, much less as a tag team. If I made a supper that my husband didn't like, he ran to my mother's. If my mother thought I was out of line, she talked to my husband. It was a losing battle.

I did find moments of temporary strength and brought up my concerns to my mother. I was met with cruelty and resistance every time. She told me that I was undermining my marriage and harming it. That wouldn't do because I had to think about my son and not just myself. According to my mother, it was her obligation to save my marriage for the sake of my son. That meant that I had to deal with whatever came along with that responsibility.

I had been a pawn in my parents' bad marriage, and now my son was a pawn in my bad marriage. That should never be the case, but it was definitely the reality for me. He was always put in the middle of the battles and forced to pick sides for the sake of harmony. When he got older, he would run to my mother for safety and reprieve when my husband and I had heated battles. My mother didn't care if it ruined our relationship so long as my son knew that Grandma was there for him—no matter what.

Few things break a mother's heart more than seeing her child run to somebody else for safety and comfort. When my son was little, it was easier to brush off. As he got older and continued to do so more frequently, it became anguishing and embarrassing. I wanted to be a great mother and love him. Didn't he see that everyone was using him? It was hard to keep in mind that he was a child and my problems were adult ones, even if they stemmed from a toxic childhood.

My mother's ruthless verbal assaults never stopped until she was too weak to speak them. She used to tell me in front of my son, "When he grows up, he is going to come live with me because I'm the only one who loves him."

Things kept spiraling into a worse situation. I wouldn't have thought it was possible, but it was. The financial situation between my husband and me was growing worse. I wasn't working and couldn't find a job. The struggles made it tough. My mother managed to help me get a job at the hospital where she worked. It worked out well for all of us because the finances became a bit easier. The person it really worked out well for was my mother though. It was one more way she had to be entwined in my every move and control my son and me at the same time. My son got to stay at the hospital daycare while I worked. That meant that every break and escape my mother could plan was spent going to be with him and weaving her web.

I hadn't fought for what I was entitled, and I was confronted by the harsh reality when I went to retrieve my son from daycare one day when I was done with my shift. They refused to let me take him because they thought my mother was his guardian, not me. I was so infuriated at everything around me because I was fighting a losing battle to show I was his mother.

My efforts to get control of my son back didn't go well. No matter how much I begged, pleaded, and tried to reason with her, my mother wouldn't listen. She took control of planning his schools, babysitters, and everything else imaginable with him in his young life.

It was a tough pill to swallow, but I felt like a surrogate mother to my own son. It was like I'd had him just to give to my mother for a present. Her control over his life bothered my father and brothers, but they couldn't do anything to change it. She was more determined than she'd ever been. I came to find out that they believed I was the problem in the situation. It broke my heart, and I didn't understand. Me, the problem? It made no sense. I ended up finding out that she had told them that I handed the burden of my child over to her and that's why they were angry. It was so annoying because they all knew, just as well as I did, how manipulating and controlling my mother could be.

One day I again discovered that my addiction to my husband had just gotten worse. I was pregnant. It was so bittersweet. I wanted the child so badly, and I longed for the opportunity to be a real mother. What I didn't want, however, was to be more committed to my husband than I already was.

After I told my husband that I was pregnant, he became utterly crazed. He ranted, raved, and demanded I abort the baby. Naturally I refused, and naturally he ran to my mother like a wounded child. I was ready for the fight this time though. I wanted the child and was not going to abort it or turn it over to my mother's control. My decision had its consequences.

My mother hit me with everything she had in her arsenal, and her pressure was unyielding. I refused to listen and stood up to her like a ferocious warrior. I was prepared to fend off her verbal daggers and resist the takeover of my decisions that I'd been experiencing my entire life. If I had to, I would have this child alone and with no help from my family. It was an unexpected gift from God and an opportunity to do what should have been done a long time ago—stand up for myself and break away from the abusive chains that had a stranglehold on me.

It all worked out. My father was kind and let me move to another one of his properties away from my mother. This meant that I could have the freedom to raise my second child without the strings of my mother attached to them. Of course, my mother ignored my second son, but I didn't mind. He was my pride and joy. There was no way I was going to let somebody else raise him because I wanted to raise him my way.

Chapter Eight
RAGING OF THE LION

There were a few key qualities that my husband never had when we were together—initiative, ambition, and drive. Despite those glaring inadequacies, I still found a way to believe he could become a provider for me and our children. He certainly didn't have any viable skills or a desire to learn them. His role as a maintenance man in the factory was satisfactory enough for him. Don't get me wrong, it's not that the job was degrading or demeaning. It was the fact that he complained constantly, but took no action to make things better.

My family financial picture was dire. Our resources were limited, and we were constantly behind on our bills. My mother would help out, but it was never out of kindness. Each time she assisted there were strings attached, and before I knew it I was a puppet that was pulled in a million different directions by the manipulative puppeteer— my mother. Still, as much as I knew that accepting my mother's help wasn't the answer, it happened. It really enabled my husband to continue trying to excel at nothing, except tormenting me.

I did win one battle, and I was so thankful for that. My mother and husband caved in and told me I could go back to school. They did mention it was just an excuse to get out of the house. Of course, that was a part of it, but more than that was my desire to improve myself. After completing my paralegal studies, I got a job with an attorney's office. It was so exciting, and I really felt like something great was starting to happen.

Earning money and being able to provide for my family was such a wonderful feeling. The easing on the financial burden should have made things better in my marriage, but it made things worse. My husband still wouldn't do anything at all unless it benefited him. The family as a whole was of no concern to him. Since I was making more money than him, he reasoned that I should pay more bills and take on more responsibility. What choice did I have but to agree? Do you think he paid his small portion though? No he didn't, and there was never an explanation as to why or where his money went.

My love for my new career as a paralegal changed the dynamics of my relationship with my husband. The more I gained success the more competitive and manipulative he became. He had no guilt or remorse for what I was going through trying to pay all the bills and hold the family together. It took a physical and emotional toll on me, and he seemed to thrive on it. Since words were no longer enough and verbal abuse was not as effective as it used to be, he turned to physical violence.

The memories of our arguments over his refusal to find a better job were vivid for years afterwards. The times he was unemployed I asked if he could stay with the boys instead of me paying for childcare. That alone would have helped out greatly. This angered him so much, and one time he got up off the couch he was slumped on and lunged at me. He grabbed my face with one hand and bit the right side of it. As soon as it was done, he apologized and watched me cry as I held my cheek. He claimed that he didn't mean to bite me so hard and was just joking. He'd only wanted me to shut up.

I managed to put that incident behind me and forgive my husband. However, I soon discovered that the incident was not isolated, but the start of something much greater in the arena of physical abuse. Our household was constantly in turmoil because of the escalated jealousy and insecurity that my husband had over my career. Every time he noticed that my confidence was growing and I was achieving something, he tried to bring me back down. Like I said, the shouting no longer worked, so he started to get more physical. He'd shove me around and watch my every move. His entire goal seemed to be to catch me cheating or doing something bad so he could punish me. I wasn't doing anything bad at all and couldn't really do anything differently.

My husband had been checking the mileage on my car and got angry one day because he said I had driven for more miles than what it would take to visit my friend. He was constantly obsessed with those types of thoughts, and it was reflected in his actions as well. When I started working in New York City, and if he couldn't get a hold of me and didn't know exactly where I was at a moment's notice, he'd go crazy with the worst of assumptions. He was out of control, and I was allowing him to be that way.

One morning he came into the bathroom while I was getting ready. I was brushing my hair, and he accused me of trying to find a man to get together with. The situation escalated, and he grabbed me by the hair and pulled very hard. Then he took the hairbrush and beat me with it repeatedly. I ended up having to call into work that day because I was in so much pain and couldn't do anything. I sat at home trying to figure out what I could do to help reassure the man that I loved him.

The irrational actions of my husband continued to worsen. I swear he just sat around thinking up things to accuse me of and waited for any opportunity to create something and cause a fight. He'd tell me that my affairs were ruining our relationship and would go off until all hours. I knew he was with other women because "I love you" messages would be going off on his pager constantly. He said that it was entirely my fault and his infidelity was due to my actions.

I grew tired of all the pain and torture. Finally, I asked him to leave because I didn't want to play his games any longer. The separation was difficult for everyone. This included the boys. Every time he picked them up, he'd threaten me and say that if he caught me with anybody he'd kill me. His ego was raging, and he threatened to kill himself and our sons one day as he took them for visitation. I was so scared and didn't want anything to happen to my sons. I called the police.

The police department was not comforting. They said that there was nothing they could do unless he actually did do something to my sons. Speculation is not enough for police involvement, but they did recommend that I get a restraining order against him.

My husband called me the same night he'd made the threats and asked if we could get together and talk. He wanted to make things work and vowed to change. I agreed to talk with him the next day. I made arrangements to have the boys go to my mother's so we could talk in private and not be interrupted.

The night of conversation and rebuilding started off very calm. We both expressed how we loved each other and wanted to make this work. It was worth fighting for. The dance of seduction felt good, and we ended up in the bedroom. Once we were in the bedroom, it was like his passion turned instantly to rage. He started screaming accusing me of being unfaithful, and his eyes were so intense and angry. He grabbed my throat and started to choke me. He yelled, "If you cheat on me, I will kill you and put a bullet up his ass. Do you hear me?"

I couldn't talk because I was being choked, and the last thing I recall was struggling to breathe until I couldn't any longer. It was a strange feeling, almost like going under anesthesia. I was drifting in and out of consciousness, and his voice was coming from a distance. I woke up and he was gone. Instead of admitting the man had just tried to kill me, I asked myself, "Why do I get him so upset?"

It took me a few days to tell anybody about the incident. I finally shared it with my best friends. They told me that I had to leave him for good. I ignored what they said because I wasn't prepared to deal with it and foolishly answered, "But I love him, and he is the father of my boys." If I would have used logic, I would have thought, "How can I be a mother to my boys if I'm dead?"

For days I had nightmares about the choking incident. I finally decided to approach my estranged husband to talk about it. I couldn't fathom that he'd tried to kill me or would want to. So when I asked, he did what he does best—deny it. He was so good at creating doubt and manipulating my thoughts. All abusers are good at doing those things, and he was no different. Since I was already afraid of confrontation, I was a victim of self-doubt right from the start and didn't stand a chance. I decided to get the restraining order. I even instructed my mother and friends that if something happened to me, then he should be investigated first.

The day that my husband was served the restraining order caused instant anger in him, which I was somewhat prepared for. He called me up and threatened that he would make my life impossible. He wanted all his belongings from the apartment and would be there to pick them up. After I reminded him that he'd need a police escort to come over, he screamed, "I will get my stuff, and I don't need a fucking cop!"

A few hours later as I was preparing supper my son came up to me cheerfully. "Daddy's here." He was so excited to see him unexpectedly. My heart was racing, and I immediately ran to the window and noticed that he was not there with a police officer, but his brother. I opened up the window and yelled out to him. "You cannot come in without the police. Go away!"

Seconds later I heard him forcing his way into the house. I ran to the kitchen and grabbed the phone to call 911. My nerves were in overdrive, and the operator seemed to be talking so slowly. "He's going to kill me," I yelled into the phone. All she kept doing was talking in a monotone voice and saying I needed to calm down and asked what my address was. I kept yelling my address and that I had a restraining order against him. I needed help quickly. The operator told me that the police were on the way and I should stay on the phone. I screamed, "I can't. He's on his way up the stairs."

The door slammed open, and he immediately grabbed me. Then he took the phone and ripped it from the wall. He started to wrap the cord around my neck, and I struggled. The police showed up quickly and forcibly separated him from me. He was arrested. The entire time this happened his brother was just casually moving his possessions out of the apartment. He also tried to take my television, and the police made him return it.

There was another officer who was talking to my boys in the bedroom. They were obviously very upset, and the officer reassured them that everything would be okay. Their father had been taken away so he couldn't hurt their mother. So many emotions were consuming me at that moment. I felt lousy that my sons had seen their father taken away in that manner. His hands were behind his back with handcuffs dangling from each wrist. I was torn between feeling sorry for the man and looking out for myself.

It's probably no surprise to find out that my mother was not supportive of my plight in the least. She'd thought the restraining order was a bad idea to begin with because his threats were not serious. According to her, it was my act of getting the restraining order that had really angered him. People in abusive situations often go wrong by not taking their abuser's threats seriously. I was no exception.

The night after the incident my mother told me that she was going to fight for custody of my sons with their father. That was such a blow, and I couldn't believe she'd do it, but she said she would. The news that she was willing to take such action devastated me. There was no way I could live without my sons. They meant the world to me, and now there was a possibility of them being taken away. Would my mother's presence influence a judge? I didn't know, and I didn't want to find out.

The next morning I woke up feeling as empty as a person could. It was as if my heart had just left my body and I was walking around in an empty shell. I was broken, drained, and felt completely unworthy. I had convinced myself that I shouldn't be a parent or even be alive—that I didn't deserve either. The dialogue I had played in my head convinced me that I would be better off not being around. My mother's words and all the incidents that I'd been through went through my mind. I was so exhausted from the fight that had been present most of my life. I'd made my mother perfect in my eyes, and her words were true. I had to admit it.

What I needed to do was find some happy thoughts to snap me out of it. I was sure of that, but it was not an easy thing to do. I knew that I had changed and that my thoughts were demons playing with my mind. I had a job I loved and my own place. My sons were healthy. There was nothing else that I should be asking for. Those factors should have been very powerful emotionally and lifted me up, but they didn't convince me at all.

I drove my sons to school and thought about how they would ever handle news that their mommy had died. My thoughts were invaded by a sinister thought: "They'd be just fine because Grandma would take them and spoil them." I had such terrible thoughts infiltrating my mind, and they wouldn't stop. I thought about how I hadn't turned out too bad being raised by my mother and that they maybe were better off with her. I couldn't stop digging the emotional knife deeper into my heart and twisting it along the way. I had never been filled with such dark thoughts before, and they were very powerful.

That day I had every intention of going to work after I dropped the boys off at school. I loved my job and adored my boss. It was a happy place for me, so I believed it was where I should be to turn my mood around. I'm not even sure why or how, but I ended up driving back home. I called a friend, and that was the last thing I remembered. I woke up in the hospital with a tube up my nose. Apparently I had overdosed on sleeping pills, and my friend had found me, called 911, and got me to the hospital. She had saved my life.

At the time, I was not at all thankful to my friend for saving my life. I felt more like she had ruined my death. I felt that I was definitely going to lose my boys for my selfish act, and I didn't want to feel that type of pain. The situation would just give my mother and husband ammunition in their fight for custody of the boys. I had made the situation worse and needed to face the reality of the situation and my demise.

That evening my mother came to visit me at the hospital. I was definitely surprised since we were not on speaking terms. When she walked through the door, I was expecting her to hit me or start calling me names. Instead, she sat next to me and held my hand. She said, "Baby girl, I'm sorry that I drove you to this. I didn't know how serious you were about leaving him. If you want to get away from him, I will help you financially so you can get away. I don't want to lose you over somebody you don't want to be with and somebody who is hurting you. Go, my child, and I will help you."

I'll admit that I thought I was dreaming or hallucinating at first. That was very unlike my mother and had a sincerity in it that I'd never heard her express to me before. Her kindness and affection actually numbed me into a state of disbelief. We hugged—a very rare event—and cried. What an awakening!

My next visitors were my boys. They were anxiously waiting to see me. They walked in with their heads down and were not sure how to react. My oldest immediately ran to me and said, "Mommy, I love you!" I could tell that they had told him about my attempt and he understood the consequences if I would have succeeded. My younger son, who was only five, wasn't sure what had happened. I noticed that he kept staring at the needle in my arm. He finally asked, "Mommy, why do you have that in your arm?" He pointed to the needle. I said, "Honey, Mommy is sick, and this is medicine to get me better." He took a deep breath and said, "Mommy, please don't die."

That evening I was in and out of consciousness. When I awoke, I realized that there was a woman in white who was in the room. At first I thought I was just catching her when she was ready to give me medicine or take my blood pressure. She had her back towards me and said, "I'm sorry to hear what you are going through. Don't feel as though you are alone." I said to myself that she had no idea what I was going through. I didn't need her preaching to me because I knew that what I had done was wrong.

The nurse continued, "It's not your time yet. You have a mission to complete, and you have not even started the journey." Now I was starting to think the lady was on crack or something. I kept talking to myself, wishing she'd go away so I could figure my life out.

She said one more thing. "You will always be guided. Just pay attention to the road ahead as lots of doors will open for you." Then she left without another word. I never got her name, but I asked the nurse the next morning who she was. I wanted to thank her. The nurse said she didn't know, but she could check my chart.

She thought the other nurse had maybe done something wrong, but I said that I'd just like to see her again.

Later that night, I was eager to see the nurse from the night before. The shift nurse came into my room and said, "I'm assigned to you, and I was here last night—there was no other nurse." I was puzzled by the revelation that had just unfolded and knew she wasn't who I had listened to. I never did see that nurse again.

It was time to leave the hospital and enter back into the world with some big decisions to make. I needed to decide what I was going to do to reclaim my life.

> *If you learn anything from my story, learn this:*
>
> Abusers live on power and ego. When they have control over their victims, it gives them more power. Abusers are hunters and seek their prey. They know your weaknesses and prepare to pounce and strike when you are the most vulnerable. Their sole objective is to conquer and defeat—you and your love cannot change them.

Chapter Nine
THE MANY IDENTITIES I MASKED

The search for my identity took me many years, and I played so many different roles as I tried to find my place. The process was not easy, but God has given me strength and I thank him for that.

The questions that people face when they are unaware of who they are swirl around like a snowflake in the wind. You wonder if it's your destiny to have more pain than joy, you question if you are smart enough to survive on your own, and you doubt every gut instinct that could protect you.

Thankfully, you *can* reach the point where you will start living the life you want. It's a matter of courage, faith, and strength to make it happen. It was important for me to talk about the many identities I masked over the years so I could understand them. I'm not alone in going through them and feeling that way. Each one was a coping mechanism and way to help me survive at the moment, but they were not good identities for creating an amazing life for me—the life I knew I deserved.

The Rescuer

My mother believed in trying to save a marriage regardless of whether it was healthy or not. She pounded that lesson into me repeatedly over the years. Although children may not understand a lot about adult relationships, they usually can tell when a couple is unhappy. It's an instinct. Some of the most obvious signs are:

- Arguing
- Fighting
- Crying
- Anger
- Depression

Those powerful emotions wear down on everybody. If children are exposed to them for a prolonged period of time, they start to believe they are natural tendencies, even though they are not.

I watched my mother sacrifice her life for her marriage. She surrendered her peace, happiness, and self-respect because she had taken the "until death do we part" vow. The fact that she was also so needy and craved being wanted didn't help her. She fell into the martyr role, and I really started to believe that her self-sacrifice was normal, even noble at times. I started to believe that self-sacrifice was the key to winning somebody's heart.

There is one conversation with my mother that I vividly remember. She told me how painful it was for her to try to convince my father to love her unconditionally and not go find love elsewhere. I could see the pain blazing in her eyes and the desperation in her voice. I actually believed that I had to save her marriage because she agreed to have me only after my father agreed to stop cheating on her. My father certainly never kept his promise, and I felt that it was my responsibility to keep their marriage intact for him.

The process of rescuing my mother left me hating my father. I detached from him, and it wasn't difficult because he was absent so much. When he would leave home, I'd follow him and tell my mother what he was up to. I found out where all his girlfriends lived and would report back. My mother used that information as weapons against my father and would spring all the information on him when she was angry.

There was one time when my mother's surprise attack almost cost us our lives. My mother went to the home of one of my father's girlfriends, and they had a big argument. When my father got home, my mother threatened to kick him out of the house. He agreed to break off the relationship with the woman. That evening the woman came to our house and set it, along with my father's car, on fire.

That night, a fireman came to my room while I was asleep to get me. All the exits to the house were blocked with flames, and he had to toss me out of the window onto a net below. The drop was two stories and completely scary. Thankfully we all escaped, but it was a truly terrifying experience.

The burnt house was not enough motivation to get my father to shape up. He continued to cheat and just went for younger women after that. He remained that way until his death.

The Bully

By the time I reached my early teens, I was in turmoil and clueless as to who I really was. My mother's constant criticism didn't help either. She believed that she had to keep such a tight rein on me, and as far as she was concerned, the best way to do that was to beat me emotionally and physically—that would keep me in line. Her actions completely backfired and did the opposite. I became so vulnerable and easily influenced by others.

Boy, I sure was a rebellious and bitter teen. I had a best friend who came from a home environment similar to mine. She managed to get straight As though, and that pleased her mother. I really liked her because she was so easy to admire. I didn't have the ability to deal with my parents the way she did. She never lost sight of her goals throughout all the chaos.

Her mother didn't like her hanging around me and was insistent that she stay away from me. It didn't faze me initially because I was growing closer to another girl, classmate. She made me feel like I was in charge for the first time in my life. She taught me how to lash out at others to feel better and release my anger. With her, I was important. People feared and respected me.

I even saw her hit her mother a couple times. That was the turning point of our friendship. No matter how angry I got at my mother, I never would have even thought about hitting her. That was absolutely out of the question. My mother had found out about her hitting her mother and told me in no uncertain terms, "If you ever raise your hand to me, I'll end up going to jail because I'll cut both your arms off. Not your hands, your arms. Then you'll never even be able to wipe your own ass again." Needless to say, my mother didn't need to say any more.

Deep down I knew that being a bully was not in me and I just didn't have the strength or energy to beat others. I could also tell that my friend was calling out for help. Unfortunately, the price of being a bully was high. I'd lost my best friend, and that meant that I had lost a truly good person in my life.

Today, we all hear stories about bullying. It's a hot topic in the news. Some kids commit suicide because they are so tormented by bullies, and pinpointing the source of these bullies' anger is difficult. From firsthand experience I know that the parents are the best source to turn to for answers:

- What is it that's making their children so angry and hateful?
- Who are their kids' friends, and how do they act together?
- What are the negative influences around their children?

For me, my bully friend was a very big influence. She gave me something that my parents didn't. In order for me to win her approval, I became like her.

There are people out there I've hurt, and I am so sorry for it. I pray they have forgiven me and that I have not caused a negative influence on their lives.

The Other Woman

When I was married to my abusive husband, I led a double life. One was the submissive and abused wife. The other was the strong, independent working woman. In both cases, I was the other woman.

My independence grew stronger when I started working on Wall Street in New York City at a financial institution. At this job, I was fortunate to be able to escape my abusive husband. Since we lived in New Jersey, he couldn't just drop by unannounced like he had when I worked close to home. His obsessive unannounced visits had cost me a my previous job at the law firm.

I used to work with a local attorney in New Jersey. However, they couldn't deal with my abuser constantly stopping by and sitting in the waiting area. They claimed he was taking up client space. I had received several warnings and relayed them over to him. They fell on deaf ears. He was so paranoid and wanted to deliberately cost me that job because he thought I was having an affair with my boss. Over the years he had continuously accused me of a variety of things that were never true. The day came when my boss just could not accept his behavior anymore and reluctantly had to let me go.

The job had been ideal for me. My boss was young, handsome, and I was eager to learn from him. He did teach me a lot and opened my eyes to the legal system and how unfair it could be at times. He tried to teach me how to be independent and create distance between me and my abusive husband. This man was the first mentor I'd ever had. Losing that job was a painful experience for me because it provided me so much.

My life as the other woman kept growing worse. I had lost my job and didn't have enough money to survive. I had to rely on my mother to help support me. I felt trapped, helpless, and depressed. It was a low moment, and my feelings of failure ran rampant through me. Here I was, being controlled by my mother even as an adult. I had become a mother, and I even discovered that my son would run to my mother for support and not me. I was losing every battle that I entered.

That's why the job on Wall Street was such a nice reprieve, if even temporary. I gained some freedom and had physical distance between me and my problems. During the day I was the independent "has it all" woman. At night I was the submissive wife of an angry, rage-filled lunatic. My husband and my mother were so similar. They bonded and became very close.

I tried to balance my dual identity for years and knew something had to change. I gave my independent woman side my all. There was no upside to life at home, but at work things were good. I was happy, productive, and had opportunity to grow. It was motivating and exciting. At first, I didn't even realize how much I loved my independence. I fell asleep excited to go to work and woke up ready to head out the door.

That independent working woman had morphed into someone I really liked and admired. For the first time, I saw what I had the potential to be, and it was really exciting and refreshing. I had respect. My views and opinions were valued. I was becoming more successful at work too. I had started out as an administrative assistant and had worked my way up to being the coordinator of custom services. In that department I got to work with the director of the department and the senior vice president as well. It was incredible.

Being in the big leagues with the heavy hitters was exciting, but it was also intimidating at times. I wasn't sure how to work with them because I didn't want to appear foolish. In particular, the director of custom services was brilliant in my eyes. He was passionate about his work and handsome. His patience and kindness were soothing, and I was beside myself. I wasn't used to receiving compliments and praise, yet he gave them to me freely and without stipulations. He was the opposite of everything that my mother and husband were.

It's amazing what a great attitude and a positive environment can do for a person. Although it had taken me a while to accept the praise and compliments that I received, I eventually did. What a welcome change! It was so great to be treated with respect and not abuse, to be listened to instead of talked at, and to have an overall healthy environment. That pride and sense of worth really helped me work hard and strive to achieve in the workplace environment. I started to learn more about myself and my capabilities. It was a very satisfying experience.

My Wall Street job was a turning point for me, and I discovered myself. I realized that I had what it took to succeed and continued to apply myself. I took more initiative, studied, asked questions, and took some courses so that I could do a better job. My efforts were noticed and rewarded. It made me feel great and vitally alive. At long last, I could also feel proud.

> *"Courage is the first of human qualities because it makes all the other things possible."*
>
> —Aristotle

Chapter Ten
DECIDING TO STAY OR LEAVE

The first step that changes the course of your life is always the most difficult to take. Once you make it and stick to it, that step becomes an empowering, driving force in your life. Once I decided what I wanted and what was worth fighting for, it all started to fall into place. I deserved a better life than what I was giving myself. I created a plan of action and followed it step by step. The first step was a dandy, and that was a painful reality. It can take years to make that first step; in my case it took eleven. The key is to not be daunted by the task ahead, but to stick to your decision and the steps you've planned. If you fail to plan, plan to fail.

After a person has been abused, it is impossible to remove all the pain. Some of it goes away in time, and some of it gets better as you start to grow into the true you. I decided to train myself to cope with my pain and discovered that I had three options:

- Become a victimizer
- Become a victim
- Become victorious

Believe it or not, victimizing others is the quickest and easiest way to escape pain. Remember the bullying route? It's the path of weakness, and it likely causes many more problems than it could ever hope to solve. If you are being abused, you may eventually realize that the abuser is weak. There is no strength of character in choosing to abuse people in any capacity. Abusers are finding a way to cope with their pain in their own selfish way—on their terms. That's why they try to subdue or dominate whomever they see as a potential threat.

You may not feel very threatening right now, but to an abuser you surely are. You have something that they want, and they are afraid to face the pain they'll feel if they lose you. You are their assurance that they can hide their pain through lashing out at you. If they lose you, they lose their patsy for the pain.

People who are in the process of recovering from abusive relationships want to start life over. They do not want isolation, but relationships that are strong and healthy. At the same time, they know that there are two types of people out there starting over to look for. They usually seek one of them out, in fact. Those people are:

1. Inflictors of pain
2. Victims of pain

If you've led a life that included abuse, you have no other frame of reference besides the two types of people mentioned above. Most people know that they don't want to be a victim ever again, and if they don't use caution, they might end up trying to find somebody they feel they can dominate. This means they have the potential to become the inflictor of the pain. That role is no better.

For me, my pain was inevitable and a reality that I had no choice but to face. I was not strong enough to use sheer force or violence to escape my pain. I chose to endure the pain in order to avoid making a difficult decision or what I perceived as a possible source of greater pain. I allowed myself to be abused so I wouldn't feel the pain of abandonment and isolation. Yet, accepting the abuse caused me great pain and isolation. I knew my relationship wasn't working and couldn't, but I chose fear instead of feeling like a failure or living in disappointment.

Fear is a driving force for victims. People allow themselves to become victims and bear the pain of losing their identity because they don't ever want to discover that they may not be loved for who they really are. Continuously entering relationships where you are a victim is a much easier choice for many people because it seems like a more reasonable choice than becoming a victimizer.

There is only one real solution—BECOME VICTORIOUS—and I'm thankful I chose that solution when it came down to it. I decided that the path of discovery and reinvention was the way to go. I deserved it, and by me doing it I could discover how to help others do it too. It is the most difficult path by far because you have to learn your boundaries, stop justifying, and create new healthy habits for positive growth. The journey has been difficult, but amazingly rewarding. Choosing victory gave me the power to transform the sources of pain in my life into tools to help me strengthen my heart, mind, and body. I live with hope and purpose. My days are exciting and filled with purpose, security, and genuine good love. The entire time this life was there for the taking, but I didn't take it right away.

Everybody has the choice to act today to become victorious where they were once a victim. Enable yourself instead of others. It is an incredible experience. You can be the person who is happy, joyful, full of promise, and living an incredible life. It doesn't have to be something that's only possible for others. You can stand tall and reclaim your life.

Our lives are what we make them. Everybody is given the ability to create their own happiness or demise. We are given one life and an opportunity to make choices every day. Do you want to squander your life with sadness and being a victim? No, you don't! Your life has value and meaning. It's yelling at you to leave an abusive situation if you are in one.

Rather than fight for their rightful lives, many people decide to try suicide as a solution. Suicide is a permanent solution to a temporary problem. These life-ending thoughts can be triggered by a variety of things, but suicide is never the solution. Never.

If you want a new, victorious life, you need to create a plan and admit to yourself that you deserve more. You do, and it can happen. The incredible journey that awaits you in life will embrace your arrival.

PART III
STARTING OVER

Chapter Eleven
COURAGE UNDER FIRE

I started paving my path to the victorious life. I moved out of state and was eager to re-create myself. I knew it would be difficult, but I wasn't fazed. The effort was intense, but following my heart and instincts paid off. The doors of opportunity started to open, and I was determined to not let fear stop me from starting over in a safe environment. Not only was this important for myself, but it was important for my children.

Life is certainly designed to be challenging and to test your determination. It's those moments that let you know you are alive and a survivor. You need to stay focused and not allow negative things to divert your intentions because that's what they love to do. I counted on my faith to keep me focused and address any negative distractions that may try to infiltrate me. I knew that I'd be better off if I took the journey and didn't wait for it to sneak up on me. So I allowed myself to go into the darkest, most destructive parts of myself until hardly any of it was left at all. I wanted it out of there, and more importantly, I wanted it to know that it was not welcomed back.

There was a spark inside of me that ignited courage to face my past and gave me the courage to heal, the ability to plan for the present, and divine inspiration to dream about the future and what it could hold if I allowed myself to learn a better way to live. It was that belief in today that helped create the miracles of tomorrow that I've experienced and continue to experience.

There was no way I could heal in a healthy manner on my own, so I got some help. I decided to get a therapist. I also knew that my healing would benefit my boys and that they also had some healing to do themselves. I was determined to help all of us overcome the negative patterns of the past and thrive in a new way of thinking, acting, and feeling.

The first sessions were all devoted to learning to be honest with myself and my therapist. It was so difficult to spit out those honest words. They made me feel foolish, ashamed, and really bad about myself. Bringing up the difficult memories from my childhood scared me because they were so painful. At times I didn't think I could handle it emotionally, but I still persevered. Eventually, I started to enjoy the journey through those powerful emotions because they helped me to reduce the heavy feeling that had been lingering deep within me. Those feelings were stopping me from achieving true happiness, and the more I released them the brighter my happiness started to shine.

My healing process was guided by three rules that I set for myself. I knew they were important and that I must do them. They were:
1. I had to be a healthy mother for my children.
2. I was not going to get involved in an intimate relationship.
3. I needed to strengthen my relationship with God. After all, I owed him the glory and honor for giving me the strength to pursue a happy and prosperous life.

> *"What matters in life is not what you do.*
> *What matters is who you become."*
>
> —Les Brown, *Live Your Dreams*

Starting over after my abusive relationship meant that I must build a new life for me. That life was going to be filled with hope because that was essential to keep me inspired by my reality. My awareness of my reality is what brought me awareness of the past bad habits and patterns that I had fallen into and allowed others to impose on me. It was one of the greatest defenses I had against falling back into the abusive cycle that I had once lived in.

As I evaluated everything, I came to realize that I had built an imaginary person in my mind and my expectation of who he should be for me. I wanted to be everything to him, but I knew that I couldn't be that any more than he could be everything to me. That didn't stop me from wanting to be the best thing that ever happened to him. After I saw the truth, I finally saw his inadequacies and the little chinks in his armor. They revealed his selfishness, and that was not something he was willing to part with. I knew I had to let him go, and who he ended up with should not be my concern. It would not help me recover and move on.

Don't Let This Happen to You!

I wasn't ready to move on until I realized and believed that I did have a greater, more empowering purpose in life and for the future. If you don't really believe it, you won't make it. It's that reassurance that compels you to keep going every day and believe that you will be successful in your goals to break free from the prison that abusive thoughts, behaviors, and patterns held you in.

Society is results-driven, and that can really mess you up when you measure your own self-worth against what you perceive others' self-worth to be. Most of us assume that successful people have it all, and we elevate them to a higher status because of their outward achievements. They become the measure for our success, and we don't believe we'll have made it until we are at their level. The true measure of a man's success is based on what is on the inside though—not the outside. What's on the inside is what is real.

Creating a new purpose in life and laying down a firm foundation was a big process for me. I jammed my schedule full with activities, hobbies, long work hours, and insane projects that kept me going until I was absolutely exhausted. I really took on a lot to create distractions that kept me from facing the things that I really should be addressing to start anew. I was busy, but I was no closer to knowing my true identity than I had been my entire life.

I needed to put a higher value on myself and my ability to succeed in life. I had to start believing what mentally healthy people have known their whole lives—you are the fruit of your lips. If you believe bad things will happen, they will. If you believe and speak positively, it will eventually come your way. If you build a house on sand it will crumble, but if you build it on a solid foundation it will withstand the storms and tests of time.

When I looked in the mirror I saw myself as fat, ugly, and unlovable. I didn't take care of my body or eat right. Exercise certainly wasn't a part of my life. I was overweight for most of my young adult life, and so I tried to change that perception. The problem was that I still saw the fat, ugly girl in the mirror. I wouldn't allow myself to see me in a new, brighter light. That constant negative reinforcement kept me from gaining any positive self-esteem or self-image of what I was, and I neglected my health even further as a result. It was much easier to hide in my thoughts of unworthiness if I looked the part from the outside.

Eventually, I decided to have gastric bypass surgery to help me out with my weight loss goals. It worked, but I can honestly tell you that I've gained a little weight back. As that has happened, I've been revisited by some of the demons from my past. I started to slowly let my victim mentality take over and cause me to feel inadequate. It took a lot of conscious work to not sink back into that big hole.

Most of us have known a woman who has negative repetitive patterns. She continuously goes for the wrong man, someone who is abusive and cruel. Eventually, a good man does come along, and she makes every excuse to sabotage what could be amazing. He's not her type, he bores her, she's not attracted, and so forth. The reality is this: she just doesn't know how to respond to a good man because she's been lost in the world of abuse for so long. How do you get to that point in your life where you admit that you deserve something good and believe it? It's not easy, but it is possible.

Chapter Twelve
SURVIVING YOUR NEGATIVE SELF-IMAGE

Self-image is the driving force behind all our actions and choices. If you force changes on the exterior without making sure it is aligned with the inside, then you become like a ship without a rudder. Regardless of how hard you work, you will end up on the rocks because you can't steer yourself in the right direction.

Before you start thinking about what you want to do or what you would like for your future, take a look at yourself. While I was going through my emotionally abusive relationship, I didn't believe what I was experiencing was actually abuse. I grew up in that environment, and I bought into the notion that it was just part of life as I would ever know it. I would focus on and notice pain at times, but overall, I was just walking through life numb from the battle.

Just imagine what it would be like to wake up one morning and have no feeling in your hands. You touch your hair, your face, and your sheets. You walk to the sink and run your hands underwater and still there is nothing—no feeling at all. If you suddenly became numb, you wouldn't be able to experience the most simple of pleasures. There would be no sensation because you would be devoid of feeling. That would significantly impact the quality of your life and cause obstacles. That numbness was my life for many years.

The numbness I lived through came from a lack of feeling in my heart and soul. The term that has been used for this feeling is emotional constipation—it blocks your emotions and doesn't allow you to feel pleasure, pain, happiness, anger, sadness, or frustration. Being abused for long periods of time makes one shut down certain emotions because they make it difficult to survive. I was in denial about it.

After I began to find myself, I didn't feel great right away. I felt a lot of pain and sadness. It caused me to cry all the time, and then the anger came. Since I'd always repressed my anger out of fear of abuse from my mother and then from my husband, I didn't know how to handle that. It was so overwhelming, but it was an essential part of the healing process. Without getting comfortable with those emotions, I could not build a healthy self-image.

There is no avoiding the healing process when you are out to improve yourself to become the person you were meant to be. I needed empowerment and the passion to pursue what was required to discover myself and my true potential. I felt there was something brewing within me. The problem was that I had never been told it was there, and I wasn't sure if I could trust my instincts.

The process of exploring your heart and starting a truthful dialogue within yourself is tough. Keeping a journal is the best way to do that effectively. I started to keep a daily journal, and it helped me acknowledge my feelings. I retraced my steps through life and acknowledged the way I felt at some of the most painful parts of my life. At times, it was difficult to not censor my writing and to stay completely, honestly raw in my emotions. Without a dire determination to be truthful even when it was scary, I'd never achieve what I needed to. I had to start accepting the fact that I was in a relationship that did cause me a lot of pain and I was the enabler of that pain.

My journal was a new relationship for me. It was one that was developed between me, myself, and I. I questioned everything and expected honest answers. Did I really want to be in the relationship I had been in for more than eleven years? Why was I with him? When he called me fatso, did I believe it? Did he tell me how much he hated me because I was the selfish one? Was he maybe the insecure person lashing out, not me? All of those questions left my thoughts and went to paper. They brought me more awareness about what I'd been subjecting myself to than I'd ever had before. I also realized that I was hurt and angry as the true answers surfaced. Actually knowing that was something new for me, and it was very awkward. Knowing that I was hurt and angry forced me to admit that I had played a role in the behaviors continuing, and I knew that I deserved better. I was not that terrible person everybody tore me down to be.

Once you say something, you can never fully take it back. It's out there and resonates through the ears of the person you say it to. That's fantastic if it is wonderful and inspirational. However, if it is something that is said out of spite, anger, or resentment, then it is detrimental and creates the very ammunition that can collapse the communication lines that make life worthwhile. That is not an enviable position that anybody wishes to be in.

Back in the day when I accepted mistreating myself, my self-image suffered. That was not the only thing that was impacted though. My self-loathing also made me feel weak, stupid, and irresponsible.

I didn't believe in myself and the ability to better myself. I realized that it was critical to treat myself with respect, and there was no other way to start getting it from others if I didn't give it to myself first.

It took enough time, but after eleven years I finally had the courage to remove the mask. The masquerade was over, and the fresh air was absolutely intoxicating. I was broke, unsure of my exact destiny, and knew that whatever came my way from now on would be from my choices. My boys would have a better life and learn how to be amazing men who were not falsely strengthened by inner insecurities about who they were. The very reasons I had stayed with my abuser were the very same reasons why I should not have given him any of my time.

Depending on your approach to accepting and taking responsibility, you will discover different things in your journey and level of patience. The important thing is that you do discover and become aware of the amazing fact that you do have options.

Chapter Thirteen
I SHOULD HAVE KNOWN ME SOONER

My determination to build my self-confidence and self-worth started with using a simple approach that would stop me from playing the victim as I had in my abusive relationships of days past.

Over time I stopped "him" from badgering me with self-doubt. There was no more "You made me do that." Phrases like, "I trust you, I don't trust him" lost their meaning. I diffused the voice of insanity that justified the abusive behavior I'd allowed in the past and said ENOUGH!

My life had contained more incidents that caused me to respond with feelings of guilt, whether guilt was a true factor or not, that I had lost my inner voice. That's bad news for anybody because it is an amazing gift from God that is designed to lead you down the right path. Ignore that voice and you will get lost in a blizzard. In my case the blizzard was abuse, abuse, and still more abuse. I seemed to plow into every type of abuse that was available. Just think of a buffet of all the worst things for you calling you in and you decide to indulge in all of it—that was me for over eleven years.

The Tips to Take You to the Top

- Never underestimate the power of your own words because they do have a lot of power. Words affect your emotional response to nearly everything and have a definite impact on your actions. Positive words will yield better things for you than your negative words could ever hope to generate.
- Try and navigate towards people who give you compliments. For me, it was my boss—a constant source of encouragement that I really did have incredible potential.
- Remember that the only acceptable response to a compliment is a smile and a thank you. Those with low self-confidence tend to automatically reply with something negative about themselves, as if they are softening the blow for when the insult arrives. Don't do it!
- Listen to your inner dialogue and understand what it is telling you. Is it creating excuses for you because you doubt your value, or is it giving you a red flag that you should really be aware?
- Create boundaries for yourself. Do not allow unacceptable behavior because you don't need it and you don't deserve it.
- Fight for your rights and don't let people trample you down. Standing up for yourself isn't always easy to do, but if you realize that it is driven by good intentions you can find the strength to do it.
- Thank God for those around you who have the guts to remind you when you need a reality check. When people remind you that you are no longer the victim and instead you are the vivacious survivor who is out there making something better, you will make it because you are living through faith and not trying to do it all on your own.

- Honor your desires in an unselfish way. You can set boundaries and make sure you are getting the spiritual fuel you need for a great life without having disregard for those around you.
- The more you work towards your goals for self-improvement the more vested you will become in them. They start to be infused into your actions, and the result is you start to create your destiny through your subconscious actions as well as your deliberate efforts.

Chapter Fourteen
REBUILDING SELF-CONFIDENCE

"You gain strength, courage, and confidence by every experience in which you really stop to look fear in the face. You are able to say to yourself, 'I lived through this horror. I can take the next thing that comes along.' You must do that thing you think you cannot do."

—Eleanor Roosevelt

The process of realizing that you need to leave an abusive relationship to pursue a better life brings a whirlwind of emotions with it. Reclaiming your life is important, incredible, and a must to have a successful fresh start. You need to get your heart in the right spot and your mind in motion to make it happen. Seeking out knowledge about your intentions and their purpose is the first steps in starting.

For me, admitting that I did lack self-confidence wasn't easy, and it left me feeling very vulnerable to those around me. I was trained to believe the abuse would be there for me every time I entered the home. That was perfectly natural because my entire life I had not known home to be a place of safety, security, and acceptance. That was not natural though; home should be a wonderful reprieve where you are unconditionally welcomed, loved, and accepted.

If you look at self-confidence as a house that has been ruined, you will see that there are two choices available to you at that moment:

1. Rebuild your self-confidence to be stronger than ever and figure out where it crumbled in the first place.
2. Just build it up as quickly as possible without evaluating anything too deeply lest it become too painful.

I chose to rebuild right away, but also to figure out why it crumbled. I wanted to overcome my pain and feelings of loss as quickly as possible. I read lots of books and made devoted efforts to improve with the help of my counselor. I made sure I embraced opportunities to be more self-reliant and less dependent on others.

The more I worked on it the more I realized the following two things that make up self-confidence:

- <u>Competence:</u> This is based on having the skills and capabilities required to do an undertaking well. Confidence comes from competence. When you know that you can perform a task competently, you're confident that you can do it. The only way to build confidence is through knowledge and experience.
- <u>Boldness:</u> Boldness is the emotional component of confidence. Boldness involves facing new tasks without fear and with absolute certainty that you can successfully complete them. It requires you to shut down your analytical mind and tap into your inner source of passion and emotional intensity.

I discovered that when doubt came into my life I needed to act boldly. Identifying my doubts and facing them helped take away the fear they held so that I could approach them in a more realistic fashion. They didn't have a chance to grow into ugly monsters because I was ready to take them on. When I believed my thoughts were valid, I'd deal with them in a more positive way. That meant they didn't get more fuel or put on the back burner.

One other important realization I faced was that I could not have boldness without competency. Bad decisions and choices that are not beneficial for long-term changes (in the right direction) come from bold decisions that are not based on solid information. Through all the books I read I began to realize that I was going to remain shaky if I didn't educate myself to be more aware of the purpose of the steps I was taking and what the correct steps truly were. Just because I wanted to take a step didn't mean that it was the right one.

The two steps for rebuilding confidence that I created for myself were to become bolder and to adopt a positive attitude. That meant no more blame game and giving my abuser power over me. I knew it would take some time to understand the process, but it would be worth it in the end. That was part of healing, growing, and ultimately prospering. In other words, I needed to get comfortable in my positive new skin because it was so foreign to me.

Jumping into action to create my departure from my old life was quite the experience. I knew I deserved better and was determined to find what "better" was exactly. Life is full of risks, and it was time for me to start taking a few for a better purpose. I couldn't be on the sidelines anymore looking at my life through dead eyes. I wanted to be alive and appreciate what was around me.

Writing down my action plan and what I wanted to do step by step was so helpful. It allowed me a way to gauge my progress and ensure that I was indeed healing. Moving away from my abuser was very beneficial because it removed the fear of abuse from my mind. I learned that it was okay to expect that I could arrive home at the end of the day and not have my world turn upside down. It could stay positive and good. I could go to sleep as happy as I was when I woke up.

Our New Home

After my sons and I moved to Massachusetts, we were completely on our own. Since I was determined to create new healthy life habits, I mixed it up a bit. We would go exploring in the car and see what we could find. Sometimes we had a destination, and other times we just went until we discovered something interesting we wanted to see. I admit, on occasion we got lost and it frightened us, but we gained confidence because we always found our way back home.

All the trips we took helped me realize that I was competent and smart. I started out small and grew as I learned and was ready for more. It was kind of like a game, in fact. We'd get lost and figure out the best ways to get back. Everybody helped and participated in finding a solution. We learned to work together and talk things out the way healthy families do.

Everything that I did had a purpose. It was either to gain confidence, create a better attitude, or better myself in some way. This new opportunity was so exciting, and I was determined to make it work. It certainly was worth the fight; plus it was great for my sons to see how a mentally and emotionally healthy adult functioned. After all, that is what I wanted for them when they became adults.

Our first apartment in our new state was not the most desirable. It was by a college and not an ideal environment for children. There were parties, and it was loud. I knew that we needed a different place. I also needed a new car because mine kept breaking down. Those things were not possible on an income of nine thousand dollars per year. I needed some new skills to start earning more money for my new start.

I went through a process of reevaluating my skill set from my previous work experience. I decided to apply for a student loan and see what happened. I got it and went back to school for computer programming. It was very difficult, but I was so proud that I made it work. My determination and fortitude to improve my life got me through it. I kept advancing towards my goals of having a better family life and achieving the things I wanted.

It's easy to understand why school isn't everybody's thing or first choice, but there is something that is your thing and first choice. You need to find what that is and make it happen when you are at the crossroads of your life. Those leaving abuse find themselves with two paths to choose from—the old way and the new way. The new way is tougher because it's unfamiliar, but once you get started you'll be amazed at how much easier it becomes.

Investigate Your Options

Don't be hesitant to investigate different opportunities and seriously evaluate them. Some of them probably seem pretty interesting and are things you should try out. Remember you can be bolder than you've been in the past—take some risks. If one doesn't work out the way you thought it would or you really don't like it, then try something else. There are so many things out there for a person to try. You just never know when you'll find the one that really speaks to you.

Risking failure is one of the bravest things you can do. Failure is an opportunity to learn and grow, so you should embrace it. Don't ever assume that you have enough boldness or self-reliance. You should be excited at the thought of challenging yourself and continuing to see what you've got.

> *The only way to find the limits of the possible is by going beyond them to the impossible.*

There are times when your best will not be good enough, but that doesn't mean it wasn't worth the try. *American Idol* is one of the best examples of that. People go on there who truly love to sing; however, they certainly cannot all sing well. The contestants are quite the collection of personalities. They strut out there in front of the judges. Some look amazing and sexy, while others embrace their weirdness, and you also see people you'd never expect would have the amazing singing voice they do. You just never know what you are going to get. It's times such as those that make you realize that passion becomes a double-edged sword.

You can definitely want certain things very badly, but sometimes they just aren't meant to be. Let's face it—if you sing terribly, your chances of becoming a famous rock star are nonexistent (yes, that may be debatable). What you need to remember is that one rejection isn't a life rejection. You can try to improve or work on the pursuit of discovering what you truly are gifted at. You cannot get everything simply because you want it.

The most amazing people who have achieved great things have failed even more. That's important to remember. It is just not possible to continuously achieve without taking a fall or two along the way. In some cases you may continue falling until you hit rock bottom and that's where you find what you were set to do all along. It's kind of like a great mystery waiting to be solved. The clues are there, and the mystery just needs a great detective—you!

I went through a series of jobs to get to something I felt passionate about—teaching. As life would have it, I had a boss at one place who was demeaning and reminded me that I was not a good trainer. Instead of slumping down in defeat, I converted her words into fuel that fired my passion to help others.

To become a better public speaker I joined Toastmasters, an incredible organization that helps people hone in on their public speaking skills. It was an incredible opportunity and experience. It helped bring me to what I do today, which is speaking to churches, prisons, and women's shelters.

You should always be gracious when accepting criticism or critiquing, even if the other person is not. You can't change their words or perceptions, but you can change how you process them and let them affect you.

A Warning About the Inevitable

When you socialize and build comradeship in the workplace (or home setting), it is difficult to stay out of the drama that many people thrive on creating in their lives. I found myself giving in to that drama at times even though it was counterproductive to my goals of creating something better. It's difficult to do, and you can't build friendships off of telling people to retrain their way of thinking to something better. Leading by example is how you show that you mean business for yourself and that you do have a better way. I learned that drama role from my mother. She was always worried about what everybody else would think and that they'd ridicule me for being a single parent. She also was known to give too much credit to other people's opinions and paid no attention to the feelings of those closest to her.

The need to please created emotional and mental turmoil for my mother. It transferred to me and heightened my sense of helplessness at different times. It was difficult to learn to decipher what was good for me and be confident in my decisions for a long time. I found that the only way I could deal with the frustration was to comfort myself with food. For the longest time I had no sense of balance in my life when it came to dealing with my emotions and the drama that they brought with them.

It's hard not to be vulnerable, and it's easy to let the negative play a large role in your life. This is one of those things that creeps into your thought patterns and mindset in the sneakiest of ways and is so tough to eliminate. It can be done though, and if you don't believe that, then it is just because it still has a hold of you—YOU CAN DO IT!

If you remember nothing else, remember this:

<u>Stop being a people pleaser.</u> Don't give in to other people's needs because you are afraid to upset them. You have needs and you should have boundaries to make sure you are not being used. Manipulative people/abusers can identify people pleasers and won't hesitate to take what they can get.

<u>Set your boundaries.</u> You need to determine what is important in your life and protect it. The best way to do this is to set boundaries for yourself and be your own boundary patrol. People will try to cross them, especially those who were familiar with the old you. You can stop that, and if people don't respect your boundaries, it's a pretty clear sign that they are not meant to be close to you.

<u>Speak up.</u> Silence is not healthy when you need to express that your boundaries are being violated or you feel you are being taken advantage of. You need to be confident that your ability to say no will not deter those who really are healthy for you. Everybody is entitled to respect, and it only comes to you when you respect yourself. People pleasing and living your life without personal regard will not earn you any respect.

<u>Talk to others in a non-confrontational way.</u> When you are taking bold steps to start a healthy new lifestyle, you need to learn how to have good conversations and dialogue with others. That means that you don't attack others for their actions. You tell them what you are feeling and what you expect—nothing more and certainly nothing less.

<u>Stand your ground.</u> You cannot start out by saying what you want and then go to feeling guilty and caving. When you do that, you've wasted your time and undermined your own needs in a very severe way. You will be tested by those around you when you first start doing these things and will turn the tide easier if you stand firm on the decisions that are good for you physically and mentally.

Chapter Fifteen
OVERCOMING ADVERSITY

"Be strong and courageous. Do not be afraid or terrified of them, for the Lord your God goes with you; he will never leave you nor forsake you."

—Deuteronomy 31:6

There are days when it feels like the distance between hurting and healing is vast; that is not the reality though. It can be closer than we think or choose to believe. Sometimes the biggest obstacle may be making the journey longer and more difficult than it has to be. Face the truth because that will make all the difference. Denial brings more pain and prolonged agony. Acceptance brings some pain, but allows it the opportunity to leave your body.

It is not always easy to acknowledge your pain. It is one of those things that you know is hurting you constantly, but you become immune to it because that is the only way you can handle it. When you feel your pain, that's the first sign that you are no longer living in denial. That is amazing and something that everybody who has been in an abusive relationship should feel—can feel.

So many people decide not to change until the pain is so intense that they cannot avoid it any longer. Then change happens because it is forced. Forced change is seldom embraced, and it is that mindset that makes all the difference in maximizing your gifts and opportunities or ignoring them and choosing to fester in a bad environment.

Adversity is the companion to change. Others who lack the strength will try to stop you. Why? They know it makes them have to face their own reality, whether they are the abuser or the victim. In due time everything does become clear, and that is an absolutely amazing feeling. That burst of positive emotional energy is one of the most poignant moments of any person's life. What makes it extra exciting is that once you experience it the burdens you carried suddenly lift from you and you know that you are free to enjoy your life. You also know that you are the captain of your ship—the one who will navigate with a steady hand through everything. God will be blessing you because you are a courageous warrior; in fact, He's your biggest fan. God put the adversity there to get your attention because He wants you to live up to the potential He gave you. His gifts are not to be taken lightly.

> *"I know God will not give me anything I can't handle. I just wish he didn't trust me so much."*
>
> —Mother Teresa

It's pretty difficult to remain calm through a storm, but it is not impossible when you dig down to the faith in yourself and God. When He holds your hand, everything wonderful is possible for you.

I recall February of 1993. I fractured my leg skiing and was in a leg brace. I was just separated from my ex-husband and was living in a third-floor walk-up apartment in a shady part of town. Several times each day I had to lug groceries or my two small children up those three flights of stairs. To put it mildly, it was a challenge.

My fractured leg didn't allow me to ride the subway, and that was the only way I had to get to work. Money was very tight, and the only source of income we had was my short-term disability insurance.

One night was particularly memorable for me. My four-year-old woke me up in the middle of the night and was crying. He said he was too cold to sleep. For two days our apartment had no heat, and our landlord was unavailable to fix it. I knew we couldn't stay with my mother, so I called my estranged husband.

I ran back to the man, despite all the lessons I had learned about his actions and their serious impact on my life (literally and figuratively). I excused it by terming the situation an emergency. The next morning I took my boys to school and noticed several police cars and fire trucks in front of our apartment. I drove up and a neighbor called out, "There she is."

A police officer looked over and walked up to me. I had no idea what I could have done and was perplexed. I looked up to my apartment and noticed that the windows were broken and the blinds melted. There had been a fire and the apartment was

> deemed unsafe. Thankfully, nobody was injured, but I found myself homeless.
>
> I didn't know what to do and decided to try my mother after all. This was her answer: "You can't stay here. There's no room for you and the kids. Go back to your husband. No one told you to leave him!"
>
> Since there were no options for me, we did stay with my estranged husband. I thought I had no other choice. It was so devastating, and I felt absolutely defeated. At first the stay was actually pleasant. We were only in a small studio apartment, but it was pretty calm. It didn't take long for my ex to start his old abusive patterns though. After all my efforts, there I was back in the same bad situation that I'd worked so hard to get away from.
>
> I finally realized that I couldn't let every setback send me running back to the life I needed to leave. I mustered the gumption to stand on my own two feet. The boys and I left again, and I put myself out there to find a better way.

It's easy to say, "Why did she go back? What the heck?" That is much easier to say than to see how courageous it is to leave—that's the part that is truly incredible and in a great way. I learned a very valuable lesson though. My instincts had been telling me all along that my old apartment (the one that burnt down) was a bad place to be. The neighborhood was drug-infested and unsafe. I ignored that because I set financial restrictions on myself. My procrastination seemed as if it would last forever, so my ultimate warrior, God, stepped in to help me make a decision. He knew that I needed to literally have the fire put under my feet to commit to trusting Him to guide me—and it sure worked! After that moment, I started to rely on Him more and walked in blind faith with Him. There's been no looking back since then.

Define Your Moment

If there is anything you remember forever, I wish it to be this:

> *You are the author of your own story. Create your own story and don't allow anyone to write your chapters for you. Stay true to your course because you deserve it.*

Follow your heart and believe. You are a child of God and not meant to suffer; rather, you are meant to contribute amazing things to this earth and reap those rewards soon after.

Made in the USA
Charleston, SC
21 March 2011